The End of Being Known

LIVING OUT
Gay and Lesbian Autobiographies

Joan Larkin and David Bergman

GENERAL EDITORS

The End of
Being Known

A Memoir

Michael Klein

THE UNIVERSITY OF WISCONSIN PRESS

The University of Wisconsin Press
1930 Monroe Street
Madison, Wisconsin 53711

www.wisc.edu/wisconsinpress/

3 Henrietta Street
London WC2E 8LU, England

1   3   5   4   2

Printed in the United States of America

Library of Congress Cataloging-in-Publication Data
Klein, Michael, 1954– .
The end of being known: a memoir / Michael Klein.
p.   cm.—(Living out)
ISBN 0-299-18870-1 (cloth: alk. paper)
1. Klein, Michael, 1954– .   2. Gay men—United States—biography.
I. Title.   II. Series.
HQ75.8.K584 A3 2003
305.38´9664´092—dc21   2003005650

Grateful acknowledgment to the following publications where parts of this book,
in different forms, appeared for the first time:
Obsessed: A Flesh and the Word Collection of Gay Erotic Memoirs:
"The End of Being Known";
Provincetown Arts: "Anonymous Life" and "A Resort for the Betrayed";
and *The Literary Review:* "A Wedding in the Sky."

For Gregg Russo, brother-in-arms, and
Ricky Ian Gordon and Marie Howe.
And Joseph Stadelmaier, Mark Matousek, and
Ariel Orr Jordan.

And especially for Andrew L. Hood,
who solved the riddle.

Deep thanks to the Fine Arts Work Center in
Provincetown and Goddard College—
two communities of artists and thinkers that have both
been homes to me for more than a decade.

In memory—Kevin Jeffrey Clarke, 1954–2002, and
Lucy Grealy, 1963–2002

Contents

Preface

I go back to Provincetown, Massachusetts, because my dear friend Gregg lives there and I always have a place to stay. Whenever I am on the crowded main summer street filled with Americans on vacation, I'm always reminded of how much I like the feeling of being sunburned and lost in a crowd at the same time and how the town runs way deeper for me than a tourist's tan. It's been my second home for more than ten years, and I wrote my first book of poems there, so the place represents a body of work to me.

I used to live in Provincetown year round, in an apartment with a skylight that had the bay rocking inside its tilted view. Now when I go and stay with Gregg—east enough from the throng—summers, for me anyway, are actually quiet at night. I have my own room at Gregg's, which I immediately close the door to after I've been there a few days, because I tend to leave trails of clothes and paper, and Gregg isn't the kind of person—part of his charm—who has to leave a lot of proof around to say that he was there.

There's a hot tub outside the house that we sit in at least once or twice a week when I'm staying on Miller Hill Road—especially in the winter, when the warmth of the water makes us forget how cold it is right on top of us. Eventually, after talking about what we've been up to in our lives, apart from each other in different towns, we usually get to the running joke: I'm the senile, retired chorus girl, and Gregg is wheeling me around the big porch of an old age home because we'll both end up—we promise ourselves—taking care of each other at the end of it all.

And I realize, a little reluctantly, every time we carry the joke into the next conversation, that it's different having a friend taking care of you (if that's the right way of putting it) as opposed to someone you have had a long-lasting, committed, and romantic relationship with taking care of you. I'm a little ashamed, I realize, that there *is* no one in the long-lasting, committed relationship department to wheel me around old age, and as the years go by, I still can't explain, in any way that makes sense, the exact *why* Gregg will be the one pushing the wheelchair into the shade.

I don't profess to be an enlightened person. So in a way, this is a book about not turning the light all the way on—a book, I like to think, about consciousness. And because I'm still thinking about consciousness as something gained during active experiences rather than anything one arrives at through hard belief, there's a kind of spiritual off-balance on certain doors I walk through in these pages, and they won't hang right and might never hang right.

The subjects here are family and love and sex and friendship, but in the story of those "spiritual" conundrums in my life, each of those wide subjects are deeply connected in surprising and unsurprising ways.

Of course, I am the product of a hot tub in Provincetown, a certain room in Connecticut, a drunken barroom in Brooklyn—or Floral Park or Elmont, New York, or Grove City, Ohio—a room somewhere, in the dizzying museum of rooms, of my parents and lovers and friends. But somewhere early I fragmented the world and its citizens. I was afraid of never being loved, so I didn't know how to ask for it. I didn't ever want to appear needy, just wise and open-minded. So like any lonely person, I experimented on people without ever intending to get hitched to one. And then I did get hitched. And then I didn't again for an even longer time.

During writing what would become a kind of riddle about sex and friendship, I thought I had to have a definitive answer to the question of why I've been outside sexually intimate relationships for so many years—not celibacy, exactly, but nothing like commitment either. I thought that by ruminating on certain kinds of sexual behavior and extensions of—or in drastic moments, remedies for—that behavior, I'd come to the great place of knowing sex and intimacy in a way I hadn't before.

But it was hard to talk about this part of life without sounding unresolved or broken about it. How reliable can a broken narrator be? And *how important is this to anybody besides me?* Why should you care about whether I'm in love or not, been in a relationship or not? And how can I write about a well of longing without ever resolving it—when I can't see to the bottom? Isn't the only real resolution just to have the relationship and get on with it? Why explore a lapse?

In talking to several people about what I was writing, I found that I wasn't alone in feeling occasionally disastrous when handling love, even though we all know that there are salient beings out there who will tell you that subjects like romance, looking for love— whatever you want to call it—is lowering the bar in literature, even for a memoir, the literary form that explores personal conflicts until they read naturally.

But relationships are where we're recognized as people who love and fail and love again. And so I've tried, through a formal invention of language and technique, as well as autobiographical rendering, to inhabit those moments of being in love or not in love—or being in *something*—with the spirit of making something strange and new.

Something Else
Is the World

We are talking about love (probable, impossible, dream), when Ruth, one of my straight woman friends (an editor at a publishing company that doesn't make any money), tells me that the best way heterosexuals can serve mankind is to make more homosexuals. She likes homosexuals. Homosexuals are the gardening neighbors on the island where she goes for the summer or the poet or writer she publishes. She trusts the homosexual because each one reminds her of a time, a way of life, she doesn't get to spend anymore— when she was new to New York, the reluctant and restless bohemian who stayed out all night and wanted to read books and drink coffee more than get caught in the good-night arms of a man she was dating.

I've never heard a heterosexual say quite the thing Ruth is saying about how to best serve mankind, so I don't know if she's being patronizing or not, but I'm intrigued by the statement. Whenever Ruth and I have lunch, I ask her about her young son, whom I'm vaguely suspicious about, and whether or not he's gay. Yet, or not.

"What are the clues, for God's sake?" she says. Well, Kate Clinton, for instance, swears it was a clue that came from her ten-year-old nephew when he announced to her, "When I grow up, I want to know everything," which I tell Ruth, turning it a little to the left, so that it comes out: "Well, you know queers are inherently smarter than anybody else."

Ruth thinks it's a funny way to look at a homosexual—as a brain—and that I'm funny for thinking that way. Then I tell Ruth that I'm much funnier at lunch than when I'm writing. Of all the things I'd like to do that I haven't done, writing something funny is right up there with skydiving. Both activities require living in the heightened version of the *now,* which is something, like most people, I project too far ahead to do.

"Maybe you want to make people cry more than you want them to laugh," she says, piercing a fried oyster with a fork the size of a crochet hook. True, probably. But if it is true, it's because I want to move them into considering something they haven't ever considered, not only make them sad. My own so-called life is the subject I can't write away from, and whatever I say about it tends to make that life sound sadder than funny. If I was a funny writer, I would have to make a lot of things up—funny memories, which, if they were really funny, I'd much rather talk about than write about. To Ruth, for instance, at lunch, over an oyster.

Or dinner. I meet my friend Mark for dinner once a week. I meet Mark because there is something exciting about his life and we are very real with each other. And he's funny. Also, Mark is extremely alive, which means he lives from book to book. Mark is always writing books. He is one of the few people I know who actually makes a living writing books, and most of them are books he wants to write.

The other books he writes — the ones he isn't interested in as much as the ones he's interested in — are still connected in some ways with how he generally thinks. Each book that Mark writes, each one that he's most interested in, has surprises in them because he's the kind of writer who tries to write in a voice that matches being alive. Which can be surprising, as you're reading along. Suddenly you'll remember life as something living rather than something that was lived.

Like many writers, Mark, in person, isn't as surprising as his writing. He's spacious though. He lets more into his consciousness than what he keeps out. He's spiritual, in that sense, without being frozen about it, without being programmatic. His AIDS has given him a rationality, too, that complements the spirituality, which I think is the reason he's been healthy for such a long time. Mark has been healthy through AIDS as it's gone from a death sentence to a chronic illness to whatever it is now. What is AIDS now? It all comes down to being able to afford staying alive. People don't die as fast as they used to, but there's still this magical thinking about it: like you get AIDS, you get on drugs, and then you're not going to die. But you are going to die. We're all going to die. I don't think we're all going to die of AIDS, like my friend George thinks we are, but so much about how we live is the result of AIDS being implicated in contemporary death—whether we die technically that way or not. Of AIDS, or not.

I asked a shrink once if he was negative and if the guy he was fucking was negative, would he have safe sex then? And the shrink said, yes, he would have safe sex. He would have safe sex because he thinks that AIDS is just the beginning, not the end, of something. He thinks that AIDS wasn't merely putting a coda on the years of sex pouring through everything, but that it built the door we walk through into the room of the way we live now.

When Mark and I get together we talk about the way we live now, which we reduce, pretty consistently, into its two components: writing and men. We always wonder where writing is taking us and why is it so fucking hard every time we begin the next thing. We are very different writers, Mark and I, but we both want to write books that have never been written before. We both want to find the thing about our lives that reads radically, that even people who don't read would be surprised by—books that don't feel like you're just reading something, just going along somewhere.

After that, Mark and I fill each other up with the stories of men—like filling up the car late at night. And then I remember that I'm empty of men now and only have their stories. And Mark remembers too. And he remembers me, standing there next to him. He remembers me being empty and never knowing me any other

way. Empty, as in: alone for so many years, in the partnership sense.

Mark asks me why. And I can't answer because I
don't know why, precisely. I had a lover for almost fif-
teen years and have loved men in the years that followed him: Gabe and Bobby in Provincetown, Pablo in
Vermont, Sam in New York. I loved men, but they
were all relationships that couldn't hold time or sex
very well.

If the definition of insanity is repeating the same
thing over and over again and expecting different re-
sults, then those relationships were insane—toxic or inappropriate or truncated. And so the closeness with the
other has always felt rocky.

Except, of course, for the first closeness I had with
my own particular other—my twin brother. I wonder
if the trajectory of that union, more than any other
family tie, has touched the way I get close to people
now. Does the twin act shine somewhere in the fabric
of being with another person because I had such an
enmeshed-with-someone-else life that every other relationship fails by nature of the fact that it could never be
as close? Liking or disliking my brother has nothing to
do with it, really. Every twin begins a life in love.

But in adulthood, I walked away from love, away
from my twin. I dropped the lines that connected us
into the seas of what didn't connect us—booze seas.
Drinking and more drinking—one of us, both of us,
neither of us. I don't know how twins work, the way I

don't know how iridescence works. I don't know how the process that finishes the iridescent material gives it the double color sense of being alive. But it does.

My brother and I don't have each other anymore. We're alone at the same movie in different cities sitting between the screen and the street. Last week, it was a Mexican movie called *Amores Perros*. I'm absorbed by my being alone as much as I am absorbed by the empty screen before the movie comes on. My absorption makes being alone feel like something I've eaten.

An empty screen is the perfect portrait of someone alone in public—nonexistent in a way, flat, reflective, gathering what's momentary about the world. Something that was once only surface becomes a deep well.

I think, before the movie comes on (three stories connected by a pack of dogs and a car accident), that it's my job—going to the movies alone, once a week, scanning the screens of my neighborhood for the history of love. I don't want other people to know how much I think about being alone or that it diminishes me or makes me self-conscious. It's my stutter, and I've gotten used to it.

And so has Mark. So I trust Mark. I think Mark will tell me something about my own life that has never occurred to me before. I think there is something in Mark's language about loneliness that might have loneliness's cure in it. I think I will be cured someday. Like everyone chronic, I believe in the cure.

Romance will be a heady ingredient in the cure.

Romance will be a main figure.

Romance will be a character of swords or cups or wands jumped out of a tarot deck.

I think there will be romance, like the psychic on Prince Street said there would be.

I went to visit the psychic right before the beginning of summer. She was famous and cost a lot of money, so it was hard to understand the walk-up apartment with the bathtub in the kitchen. Maybe she was saving all her money for a trip to Mars or, like the famous story about Bruce Willis, keeping this apartment the way he did his old apartment in Hell's Kitchen, as the *before* photo to see where she came from.

The psychic told me I will meet the love of my life outside, and when she said it, I thought she must have been getting my past and future mixed up. *I already met the love of my life,* I thought—in the ago-life, the Life of Richard. It happened already. Isn't the reason you go to a psychic to confirm that nothing really ever happens again in order to make room for the one thing that has never happened?

According to the psychic, I will go back to the future. Romance will be drinking coffee, and I will be laughing. At some point, romance will say, "But that's not funny. It's not funny that I love you. I'm being serious and you're being funny. You don't have to be funny. I would love you if you weren't funny. I would even love you if you were sad." I am funny and sad, like most of the alone.

The psychic says romance will live by the sea, which is sad, in another way—in the eyes, from how the sea goes into them and, in his case, makes them blue. The whole new life, including the sea and me at the sea, is somewhere down a long road, the psychic says. It's in my future—something I don't have that is made of me.

"There's nothing you can do now about what hasn't happened to you," she says, as though I'd forgotten how, during most of my life, I've managed to live as myself.

I sit in the psychic's kitchen drawing a little protection around myself—like a hospital curtain. Let's say I am in the hospital after a crack-up about being alive. But the crack-up is mostly about being alone. I tell the shrink that comes every other day that I think of the sexually intimate relationship as an amount of money I already spent on one man. Money can't buy you love, especially when you don't have any left.

But why am I broke? I loved relationships. I loved sex. I loved talking to my lover in the horizontal position. In the horizontal position words and breath sounded the same, especially when there was booze in them. Then I stopped drinking in 1984. Other people who stopped drinking will say the answer to my solitude begins and ends there. But I downplay sobriety's effect the way the active alcoholic downplays booze. If you had my life, you'd drink too. And if you had my alcoholism, you'd have gotten sober too. Or die.

I didn't die. So I should be free. I should be free as the lucky ones who pulled through the dark night of the soul. Lucky us, the lucky ones. I should be singing under the lucky stars that fill up the dark with the rest of dark's chamber music. I should be thriving in the reprieve-life. I should be spiritual and grateful to someone or something. Someone or something saved a wretch like me. I'm really something. I'm a comeback.

But like the comeback, I'm wobbly on stage. I'm too busy remembering what it was like then instead of letting it be what it is like now. I'm foggy in sobriety. I'm foggy around my heart. I'm foggy with real feelings. Somebody told me on the day of real feelings—the day I realized that the world didn't have enough alcohol in it for me to drink—that it was all about real feelings now. I haven't figured out the heart's rewiring, exactly. I don't know my sober heart because it's used to being deceived. My drunk heart couldn't tell the burning of love from the burning of hair.

I have nothing to compare sobriety to except its blatant opposite. Something wonderful and awful happens at once when you arrest alcohol. The wonderful thing is you get your life back in one piece. And it's a whole life left over from an empty life, and you have no idea how to maneuver it. You have to go learn everything again. Everything comes back in the same order it disappeared. Your life starts up again like it did when you discovered drinking, but of course, it's a different life. You become conscious at the bridge where you lost consciousness. You realize that you had to drink to get sober.

People who never drank aren't sober: they're just alive. I can't compare being just alive and sobriety. I can't compare sobriety to what I was like, or what *it* was like. The world was something and something that happened to the world. Like me. I was a writer who drank. And it took a while for writing to come back when I stopped drinking, because writing makes you disappear. In the beginning of sober life, you are too busy appearing to disappear. Disappearing isn't mindful. You're afraid to disappear because you haven't felt this alive for a long time, and you don't want to *miss* life anymore. You feel good about living. You finally get it about living. You *just live*. That's what you do without alcohol. You live without alcohol. You live and live and live. Then, in moments of love or suffering, you remember living.

I used to complain a lot to fellow recovering alcoholics about living. What it was like. I used to say that I wasn't creative anymore. I was just a soldier who showed up. I didn't have a cock. I wasn't gay. I hated sex. I was a worker among workers. Being sober meant being *straight*. It took a long time to get naked with a man again. I bemoaned the time it took. I don't like time, which is why I never drank scotch. Scotch is an acquired taste and I was in a hurry. I drank beer. Beer went down like a switch. After stopping drinking beer,

I didn't want the contemplative life. I didn't want to be still. I wanted to move. I wanted to stay up. After five years sober, I bitched about being single a lot. My roommate said, "That's right, blame your sobriety." My roommate thought clarity was as debilitating as drinking thinking. If you asked him, he'd say that sobriety wasn't any *better* than alcoholism, just its flip side.

Before Mark and I leave each other, he always says a variation of, "I just want someone to put their arms around you." And I love Mark for bringing the variations, like flowers. The variations are strewn at love, but they also remind me of the wholeness inside someone's arms. Arms are the ultimate prize. Forget about my talent for being alone. Forget my pulse of self-esteem. Love blooms in the arms, in the bouquet of space. It blooms when there's *someone actually there*.

And in the last almost twenty years, only one relationship has come into light, but it kept flickering. It was called Sam, and it swung its broken light across the horizon like Morse code. Sam kept forgetting about the future, because whenever I said we were in a relationship, he said it was not a relationship. It wasn't a relationship because he didn't like relationships. Sam couldn't find the part of his homosexuality that had someone else in it. Sam was monosexual. When we were having sex, he didn't want to see me socially, and when he saw me socially, he didn't want to have sex. Sam split me up, like a tour's itinerary. The tour led us to a field. There was nothing growing in the field. It was a field of time. It was a zone. We were waiting for the millennium. Some people thought all those millennium countdown clocks were nuclear devices. Some people were afraid of the millennium because they thought it was going to mean the end of the future, not the beginning of it. Which made it sexy, and made you feel like going out.

Sam and I went out on New Year's Eve. He wore a leather bomber jacket. I wore a leather bomber jacket. We leathered together. But leather couldn't keep the sex consistent. It was tumultuous and unpredictable sex. Unsafe safe sex. Sam never knew what unsafe, unsafe sex was because he was always afraid of sex, even before being afraid of sex was a consciousness. Then he thought you could get AIDS in a kiss. So he didn't kiss. Not deeply. He thought something would get inside the kiss to darken it, catch in the throat and cancel love. He kissed like a man who was afraid of being remembered for the way he kissed.

I didn't know very much about Sam except that he was staying put for a long time now—playing dead, in a way—in the same kitchen for twenty or so years, cooking five-alarm chili. He's never equated love with being happy, the way I do, or did. But I loved him because he was brutal and tender like men I have loved, and he was attracted to aspects of my physical self that I've been most self-conscious about—on-again, off-again weight, hair everywhere—a bear, I am, but never one who belonged with the bears.

Sam was tall, celebrity handsome, close curly hair, and eyes that were magnetically blue. The left side of his chest was caved in from a lung operation, which seemed to be the only interruption in a consistent life of going to Italy every February; of working at the same place for ten or more years; of seeing his friend Louis on Wednesdays; of driving an old lover's car out to East Hampton every Saturday just to have his one night with anonymity, at the sea.

Sam was consistent, like men I wasn't used to loving. And even though his consistency would never lead into something solid with someone the likes of me, it made him evenly distributed. The small fires of anger or impatience that would break out occasionally were almost always well contained or quickly extinguished, which made every time I was with him funny and open and sexy. And he could, almost as a side note, be haphazardly romantic. He said it never mattered, for instance, what table we sat at in a restaurant as long as, "I'm across from you."

But Sam made romance a treacherous path to nowhere, so that whenever I felt his warmth as a signal bringing in the frequency of love, he pulled romance up from under me. He tore up the contract. He took back his occasional relapses into affection and sexual attraction. Whenever I brought up the future, he flattened it. He may have been living in the moment, but he kept repeating the same one. And so I stayed in the middle of what he was and what he wasn't, not knowing exactly where we were heading because each of us was going to get to the future without each other. I left things alone. I ate big crumbs. I didn't get what I wanted. And I didn't give back what I didn't want.

I didn't get what I wanted partly because neither of us really allowed ourselves to know each other erotically. We *remembered* sex. So fucking was fixed instead of mercurial. We performed for each other until we were left adrift somewhere near pleasure, but nowhere near real intimacy, much in the same way an anonymous partner remembers your cock instead of your touch or the taste inside your mouth. I didn't know a lot about Sam's sexual history. It was obscure, like skim milk. I was obscure. Whatever turned me on sexually was obscure. I didn't know how to ask for something specific in bed. I didn't know how to negotiate. I fell asleep during the meeting. Whenever a man before sex would ask me what I liked, I immediately thought of a favorite piece of music or a book. I didn't think of likes and dislikes in a sexual context. I thought sometimes that what I really wanted was everything I never allowed myself to have in bed — talking dirty, bondage, toys, food, two people instead of the one. S/M. I'm somewhat conservative when it comes to sex. I didn't know you could have a sexual taste. I couldn't remember if sex was evolutionary or just kept being reinvented. Then safe sex made sex evolutionary. Sex — out of the past.

One night, Sam and I took a cab after a play, and I kept my hands moving along his inner thigh so many times that the cotton started to feel like paper. Then when we got home, Sam was exquisitely commanding in bed. Not in a goofy way. Not in a putting-on-a-character way. He was commanding in the sense that this is what he did and he was good at it. This very thing. He wasn't fucked-up about sex the way I kept telling him I was fucked-up about sex before this night of not being fucked-up about sex, in the before-life of incest, booze, the whole choir of contemporary excuses for not getting it up. He knew there was a way inside me that no one had bothered trying before. So he tried. He tried to fuck me; then he fucked me. And he knew how to fuck me so that my power surged up alongside his power. This was something I didn't know about him, until I thought about it later when I was touching his lips with the smallest point of my tongue—kissing until we reversed. Then I thought, *Now I know this about him.*

We were moving forward instead of just across. We had been moving across for a long time, across the shiny surface of ideas but doing nothing—nothing flying, nothing landing. My lover that night was a surprising, kind, attentive commander. His commands were not about violence or about a kind of sex that, if you turned it over, bad stuff from the past would fall out. His commands were about tenderness and giving pleasure to the other person. I didn't think I liked that—so many commands, so much talking, so much focusing on me and not enough on him. I didn't think I liked the sentence, "You'll do what I tell you to do." But I liked that sentence. I loved that sentence as it fell in so much black and white out of his red mouth into my mouth.

I loved that sex was so new and that I didn't know it before, that I hadn't trusted it—the full conjugation of trust as it takes in another man. So we came up, rocked up, up on our knees—the rocking made of the fucking and the break in the fucking. The fucking was intimate, clinical, intimate, clinical. Talked about. The talking was loving, rude, loving, rude. The fact that there was language—a script of light, the sweat, then come across his chest and then the come thickly running down until it filled the tender pool, cross-hatched with light branches of hair, across his navel.

Desire was a chain of commands in the absence of events.

He gave me pleasure with no thought of his own pleasure.

He didn't talk about pleasure as it pertains to a person. He talked about pleasure in being of the world. Of wanting one thing.

Then there was just pleasure, itself, alone, floating past us.

He was finished making love to me and I was finished making love to him. I was lying there—a muscle of repercussion or shipwreck of blond hair and come and lube and ashes.

An exercised heart.

Thighs.

Inner thighs.

Sweat. Ashes.

The ashes weren't real, but they were known.

The ashes were from rising up again and again and again and again and again.

A week after Sam fucked me the first time, he asked me why I didn't believe in safe sex. We were standing in front of a Starbuck's, like the rest of New York, waiting for it to stop raining. I was walking Sam home, which also meant that I wasn't going to sleep with him that night. Walking Sam home meant that I would leave him by his door next to the hardware store and dreamily catch a cab, wondering for the umpteenth time how the relationship got to *this* peculiar place after it had been in the more spacious place of him cooking dinner and asking me to take off my clothes before we were finished eating.

"What are you talking about? Not only do I believe in safe sex, I actually practice it."

"You let me fuck you without a rubber."

"Actually, Sam, that's not true. Don't you remember I told you to put on a rubber if you were going to fuck me."

"You did?"

We got caught in the rain a lot. We were suited for rain, this *thing* of us—a curtain of sad and heavy and sexy rain. I fell in love—some version—but I was the only one who wanted to walk across it. Sam wouldn't acknowledge anything emotional in him or what he might have sensed was emotional in me. He wanted to be loved but didn't want to love. It would be easy to call him a narcissist, but the modern narcissist still needs a sideman to activate the gaze, and Sam didn't believe people had that much effect on each other. Sam had a loner's consciousness. The company of other men wasn't the arena in which he thrived. When Sam was alone, he was integrated, and when he was with someone else, he scattered himself. He wasn't extravagant enough to have feelings *and* physical desire. He split it up—the body and the story about the body. And so sex gradually went out of our relationship like summer out of the sky.

Then Sam feared me. He feared me without my cock. He feared me when I couldn't get an erection. He couldn't talk about it, so I didn't talk about it. Sometimes I think sobriety has turned me into someone without a cock—an ordinary citizen, someone appropriate, who does the appropriate thing. When I got sober, I didn't go to the hardware store anymore to buy an orange, in other words. But I also didn't know how to be in love, in sober time, and that is what I really wanted to know.

When I fell in love at nineteen, I thought it would last. But if it didn't last, it would at least put me on a wheel of the everlasting. Something constant was going to happen. I was going to be remarkable. Love was going to be this extreme pattern. And the pattern would bring somebody. Then I would lose somebody like everybody losing somebody. Then I would have somebody again after losing somebody. In this way, love would make me a type, make me continuous, but also give me an expiration date. I would know death better because of the expiration date. Death wouldn't be the end of life but the end of love. I could always live without *feeling* life (what being drunk did). I could live, did live, right up to the edge of not living. Lush life.

In the Mexican film *Amores Perros,* love makes corruption very lush. Each person in the movie has a dog they love—more, in a lot of ways, than a person they love. But the dogs, in the lives we think they are having, hate each other. So the movie drives along a lot of dog-fighting landscape. We are in Mexico City. Each dog dies except the one who can kill the other dogs. Then the main killer dog decides not to be a killer. The killer dog decides to just love. It's the dog that goes on the hero's journey, not the person of the dog. The dog goes into the sunset with the man, into love. Violence and love go in the same container.

I remember love. And I thought I was good at being in love. I thought there was a lot of room to being that. And I loved how loving the beloved fanned out into the world body. I loved how light from everywhere else fell in my lover's hair. I loved how the night seemed to dampen it. I loved how his clothes loosely fit his body's idea. I loved how easy love was when it hadn't been easy. I thought hard about love growing up, because it kept making the branch tap on the window. Then I thought about the branch in a storm and how the wind and dark water would make it swell into a kind of force—love was like that then—a force to be reckoned with. How was I going to bear it?

My mother loved me, but she was damaged for so many years. She suffered from depression. In those days they didn't have enough chemicals for it, and my father would have to drive her in the summer to electricity—shock treatments—once a week. Then, my mother never found the right drug, so she tried all of them. My mother had to learn how to love everybody on each drug and how much of herself to let out. Love wasn't really an aspiration with my mother as much as it was the effect of a mood's surprise. Then I loved her.

My mother used to say, "Trouble floats." And there was a static cloud of pill powder over her life. Pill powder lined the bottom of my mother's purse and the pockets of her mink. And I wrote about the powder, which brought up love. That was the actual invention of writing: love.

Then I fell in love with another person, another man. And wrote to him. Writing was how the relationship sailed across the physical. I wrote songs in the morning and drank coffee and cognac. My lover was building a floor. I wrote one song every day for as long as we were together. Which was a whole life. I wrote music to accompany something my lover kept bringing into the room with him. I was a grown-up.

And when I was grown-up for awhile, I loved the sheer physical being of love. I loved the tense but elastic pull love had on me and the physical body. I loved feeling like I was being *turned into* love. I loved my lover's erection and how it had become a specific physical thing about living in New York in 1975 at 415 West Forty-seventh Street; how being in love with him created the new and strangely riveting desire of wanting someone to be literally inside of me. I never had had anybody inside me. I didn't have enough space inside me before I turned into love.

I was a drunk in love with someone.

Now I am not a drunk who is not in love with someone.

A Wedding in the Sky

One night, some members of my tribe and I were sitting at a marble tabletop in a romantic restaurant, which meant that we couldn't see each other. It was dark light, so we talked about love.

Then we were talking about what it is like to have a specific love for someone you haven't met yet. The context was that one of us wanted to adopt a child. I suddenly remembered children, the way they are in my life sometimes like dividers in a notebook. It used to be that you could tell children what the future would be like because so much of what already happened would be in it. The future would just be the next installment of what couldn't stop happening. Then you could teach children what was simply waiting for them. They would join a dance that had been going on for such a long time in the old city. They would just lengthen into what was already, what you knew, what your parents knew. They would just add themselves like beads on a cosmic necklace. The old world.

The world didn't change very much then. Time was still linear. Time was still there, like a quality. Then, a speed. This is the first time in history we are teaching something that won't necessarily go forth. And so we're lost, in that way. We're wired, but not inspired. We're virtual. But still, I love. Or forget that I love, where it comes from, why it's always so fucking moving. I've come to a kind of between place, as hard to gauge as a meadow in the sky.

I still love in the old queer way. But too much about queer life is bereft. I'm not tired of being gay, but I'm tired of everybody else just discovering it. Mainstreaming thinned us out. I miss the margin. I miss fighting. We're like everybody now. We're vain. We emphasize what's popular. We talk about famous people. We're too beautiful on the outside. We flee to ghettos for vacations.

Yesterday in the Provincetown ghetto, J.T. and I were talking about romance. I know J.T. because of some radar we both share. We're connected by an inap-propriateness. Sometimes we fall in love with friends. Bobby was a friend I fell in love with once. I fell in love with Bobby in the middle of a New Year's Day kiss. We drove to a beach in Truro. Thomas Merton said Truro sounds like a word that means the loneliness at the edge of the sea. I understood Merton's sentence so fast the day I kissed Bobby because of the idea that a kiss is one stage away from loneliness and one stage toward loneliness. Bobby's kiss was proof of what had been in the air for a year. His kiss happened after it was in the air for so long with the light and the dampness from the sea. I fell for Bobby in a room next to the sea.

And watched Bobby as he wandered into an AA meeting. He looked like the painting of the priest hanging in the middle of the room. The priest was beautiful, but a little haunted like he had seen the wrong death—that the death he saw would not let his life fit into it. Bobby looked broken spirited too. He was a rumpled and beautiful character out of a Dostoyevsky novel. Rogozin, I think it was, from *The Idiot.* It was winter, so Bobby was bundled on the outside. Then his heavy gray wool overcoat gave way to a T-shirt and shorts. He was lean and Mediterranean handsome and looked like summer—which means that, since it was winter, he was someone dressed for a dream.

I was drawn to Bobby. Badly. There was an obsession percolating, which meant that I was making Bobby up before knowing who Bobby was. I was attracted to what drew Bobby: the sea there and the men and women huddled around the coffeemaker. I was thinking, while I was standing there with the drunks, that I have always been drawn to men who don't dress for the weather—men who are in the world but not wholly of the world. Dreamers. The job of the world where the dreamer is concerned is to interrupt him with proof.

But Bobby fought back. Bobby tried hard to stay in his dream. He was committed to it. Then one day, he sat in a chair next to me with his cock hanging out. He had a very provocative relationship to his body and to sex. And so his body was very beautiful. Every limb had the same amount of conversation in it, which made it more personal than other beautiful bodies.

Once, a long time after this, I saw Bobby driving in a car with a new boyfriend. When they got closer I could see that they were both naked. Jack and Bobby were driving down a crowded street in the middle of summer—a street from a dream. Dream Street. Jack stopped the car and Bobby climbed out through the window and sat on the hood for a minute, for a reaction. Then he climbed back in. It was too funny and out of context to be sexy. But then it was sexy, too, because it was him, and this was the way Bobby liked to be in the world. Before the car and the boyfriend, Bobby sashayed and walked down a dirt road every Monday night, away from AA and all its principles, to me where I lived in a little studio on Atkins Lane in Provincetown. There was a skylight that was flush with the edge of the sea. I could smell the sea on my sheets. And the sun was there, too, mixed up in the sea smell.

Bobby talked about his acting career gone bust in New York City. He went to graduate school and joined a theater company. Then Bobby met an actor/addict whom he loved. Then Bobby drank. Bobby came to Provincetown to find sobriety. Bobby didn't know that the sea wouldn't automatically give him sobriety, but we both knew there are days when the sea can look like being sober.

There, there, there. Calm, with the old terror under-neath—like any mirror.

One Monday Bobby and I were wrestling on my bed. We were playing a game, which always lets you know a little more about a person, so the rhythm of who we were was changing into other ways we've come up with to live. The game floated merrily along with the psychological. It was a serious and funny game that started out being a game like the towel snap in the locker-room game. Or the pat-on-the-ass game. It was a game that is never read as sexual, although it could *only* be read as sexual. I touched Bobby's chest and stomach through his inappropriate clothing and named his chest and stomach. I named his arm and inner thigh. And when I casually lay my hand across his crotch, I decided to let him name it. Bobby whis-pered, "And that's Bobby's penis."

I think this was falling in a heap that comes after roughhousing instead of love. It didn't have the little coma that comes with love. It felt like something that was always there and we were just putting a game next to it. We were tender like wolves. Or accidentally tender, like a tooth loosening. Then in the space be-tween the accident and the tenderness we recognized each other as gay men who were brothers in recovery. The touching game was more like sweetness than a direct invitation into bed, but it stayed with me for a long time. It stayed with me long enough to become rhythmic.

But it was still the troubling theme that never leaves a story. When the opportunity arose every Monday night to go back to that touching place, it would be skipped over because we didn't want to have the wrong idea about each other. So I despaired whenever Bobby left to walk the beach back to the house he was living in, because I knew that to reach my hand deeper down than his crotch and into his love life wasn't something he needed in early recovery. But I wanted Bobby. I wanted my friend. Then the New Year's kiss happened, and so I thought it meant that Bobby and I were sliding away from friendship into the unknown where the little coma happens. Then the thought came to me that we could be lovers, that we were on our way to being lovers. Plus, I loved him during all the stages of loving him.

Two weeks later Bobby went to New York, and I called to tell him that I wanted to be lovers. He was shocked by my desire and suddenly confronted with desire, or whatever amount of it was left after my news neutralized it. Once love was put into a context, it was patented, which was hard for Bobby. The kiss was in a dream, and the boundary between friend and lover wasn't strong enough to stop us. Bobby wanted to remain friends—friends who kissed and had sex every once in a while. Then after that, we had sex every once in a while. But the confusion drained the relationship. I kept showing up for the dream kiss from a man who didn't want me in his dream.

I couldn't see clearly. I knew early on—the way one always knows early on—what was possible and impossible in terms of love and Bobby. I knew that we were both playing a kind of game and that I was accepting love in its constricted form, which it doesn't actually come in. I wanted my friend because, like all obsessives, I couldn't have him. But I wonder how much of myself I wasn't letting *him* have? And how much of *that* was love?

Two years later I found myself in another friendship that turned its head to face the same weak boundaries of friendship or love. We were outside a cabin, on a lake, on a dock, in midsummer. His name was Gabe, and we had spent the early part of the summer in a bearable heat wave at his family retreat, which was a funky cabin right outside Boston. The cabin was a few exits down from an infamous rest area. Gabe called the cabin the Fort. The Fort was hidden by the trees and pitched on the top of a slope that reached down to Spectator Pond. Days circled around the pond, and nights, when the pond was too dark for swimming or boating, circled around a parking lot at the mall. At the mall, we went to the movies with the rest of America. I was falling in love with Gabe during the story on a screen in America.

I tried to keep the love away because he was a friend and had been a friend for too long for everything to change suddenly into the other kind of love. I didn't know how to tell Gabe that my heart had grown specific around him. But what's the rule for such things? Is there an expiration date for romantic love? If you don't make your intention known with someone soon enough, does the friend automatically take over and push the man who wants sex aside? Why don't men ever ask, in the beginning, what kind of relationship we want it to be? How long does being a friend stave off Eros? Why can't you have sex with someone you've known for years?

Every man I meet in the beginning is a potential sex partner until the sense of the erotic is neutralized by a hope for the future. I don't know how to act all the time. I don't know how to seduce or look for clues or ask the right questions. In sobriety, I'm in the same room with intimacy, but I'm never used to the light.

In the beginning of our relationship, Gabe was picking up guys, having sex. I was celibate when I moved to Provincetown. I didn't cruise at night because sex was too much in the air. The air made me disinterested. All I wanted to do with the air was breathe it, not get all sexed up about it. I wasn't pushing romance that summer. But there were feelings *around* romance, *around* possibility, that went toward Gabe. I wound and wound and wound the feelings around Gabe to see how tight they could get. In this way, I was involved with a possibility. I wound and wound, and then I talked. We talked. We talked in his truck and in his kitchen. We talked in his bed and in his garden, where some rabbits were. I came to appreciate Gabe's heartbreak and vulnerability. He had been abused. He was in recovery. His recovery made him financially successful, which surprised me, the way it always surprised me—money enough for more than enough.

And he was fractured, but whole inside that fracture. His fracture kept healing, which gave him an effervescence. And his effervescence made me vibrate. We slept together without having sex, and his effervescence was in the bed with us. Gabe used to shine. Gabe was alive when he shouldn't have been. Because of the recovery, Gabe was alive. Especially in summer.

We lay naked together on the dock and talked. Or we got in the canoe and moved around the lake in slow circles. We sang Joni Mitchell songs, and Gabe turned me on to Tori Amos, whom I liked. Tori Amos sounded good on water. Late lake music. And that lake had a kind of hum that typified summers for me. The lake brought down a drowsy band of sunlight that got interrupted by a smaller summer of crickets or laughter.

Gabe and I had perfected the canoe in Provincetown the summer before, when we used to make Sunday sojourns out to Long Point. There were a lot of dolphins that summer, and after the dolphins, we got out of the canoe and collected sand dollars. There were a lot of sand dollars that summer too: lots of riches right under the surface.

Then an extraordinary hurricane happened. Gabe and I were there on earth simply to look away from it and up at the sky—which was particularly startling, black blue, full of stars. It looked like the sky from Luis Buñuel and Salvador Dali's *Un Chien Andalou*—which dissolves into a woman slicing her own eyeball. But this sky—Gabe's and mine—had been swept clean after a hurricane without rain turned it upside down and knocked out the electricity in Provincetown. The summer business—the heart of economic life in the town—stopped, along with the heart of a photographer in the East End after his house fell in around him.

At night, real night, Gabe and I took our flashlights and cruised Commercial Street in the dark. We kept the flashlights off until someone passed who we intuited might be attractive, and then we turned the flashlights on and seductively asked, "Are you cute?" But it was hard to cruise guys with Gabe, even in the dark, because I wanted to be cruising him.

Hurricane Bob hit the town hard enough for a T-shirt to be written about it: *I was blown by Bob*. And I watched most of the storm through the window of Gabe's house—an intermittently shaking house on a high point of town—reading Patricia Bosworth's biography of Diane Arbus and thinking about the one time I met the photographer and knew, even then, standing outside her oncoming fame, that she was utterly unique. Arbus had just gotten a pair of X-ray glasses— the kind you send away for with a coupon from the back of a comic book. The glasses were supposed to give you X-ray vision, and she was looking *through* her hand as she held it up in front of a table lamp.

As turbulent as it was getting outside, it was also perfect napping weather—or weather for construction paper, scissors, and glue or soup. Before the storm, Gabe cut out the sunflowers from his picture-perfect garden and set them on the kitchen table. The brilliant stalks were bigger than the vase they were standing in, and watching Gabe with the sunflowers, I realized I've always envied men who have been able to navigate those parts of being alive that *only* have to do with re-membering how to finish something—daily rituals that keep the *personality* out: baking, planting seeds, raising rabbits, making furniture. I lived with an archi-tect once who used to take my breath away by taking down a wall.

Occasionally we ran outside to feel the storm against our skin, to be *in* something like that—an act of God—to feel an act of God pushing on our minds. The sky had grown so colorless that we were in outer space even more than usual. On another day, there would be nothing in the sky to refer to the fact that we were moving at all—except a cloud or two. But on that day, antennae were moving against the colorless sky and roofs were flying and boats out in the bay were fast going under. And then it became a storm that seemed to have a distinct target in mind: the trees.

In the front lawn, limbs and leaves got mixed up with a fence. A telephone pole at the end of Pearl Street fell into a power line, which suspended its crash and kept it from going through a roof. So many leaves smashed into fronts of houses, windows, and cars that the street looked camouflaged. And the sound of all this: puffing and sucking—the sounds of centrifugal force. The most spectacular sight I saw was in front of the 1807 house in the West End. A huge elm uprooted along with half the right side of the lawn. It pulled the roots up four or five feet, taking the lawn with it, so that hedges were turned almost vertical.

In the week after the hurricane, the sound of the wind and the rain was replaced by the sound of generators and applause from people in the street whenever a Com Electric truck would roll by on its way to restore power to so many powerless houses. Lights finally came on in the studio where I lived, which was situated in back of one of the only houses in Provincetown that had two chimneys. One chimney went when an elm fell on it, the other a few days later when, in a tree-cutting mishap, a huge limb swung out of control, knocked the other chimney over, and sliced through three Georgian columns of the house across the street from where I lived.

The tree company didn't come back until the next morning to finish cutting the whole tree down. Then they cut it in tire-sized sections and stacked them in the garden at my front door. Jackson Lambert, married to Carmen, owner of the property, restacked the sections of the tree late in the afternoon so that it looked like the original. His memorial to the savage hurricane beauty, I suppose. And in front of the house, Carmen left her memorial: a pink rose in a glass jar that sat on top of the three-foot stump—all that was left of the tree that had given the house so much shade. It was mild that day, and the wind blowing through Carmen's flower wasn't strong enough to turn it around.

After the hurricane was finished with Province-town, Gabe was somewhat finished with me. He found a real lover and disappeared into him, into the country, into his own business, and into what would become our last summer together. And I remembered what I had promised my friend, Michael M., before he died— that I would try and succeed, like Dr. Frankenstein, in making a monster of love out of equal parts: Michael M., of course, and everyone else I loved. Gabe and Bobby were added. Which is what I was telling J.T. There was this certain storm of love: the story about falling in love with friends. Which became *this* story about falling in love with friends.

J.T. and I were standing in the chrome reflective sea of cars in the parking lot at Herring Cove. The air was filled with wet salt and beach roses. The sun was drenching but specific. I was ready for a conversation in which I would really have to pay attention. I've never been much of a beach reader. I'm available. Or I'm in a play. Sometimes my friend Al and I take copies of *Who's Afraid of Virginia Woolf?* to read out loud. We would grab a couple of beautiful boys and force them to read Nick and Honey. As George and Martha, Al and I al-ways up the stakes of the script a little. We flirt with

Nick and Honey a lot more than the stage directions call for.

There's a famous old rumor that Edward Albee originally intended the play to be performed by four men. But we can never imagine it. It would make the play sound ridiculous. It would make the play be about men kibitzing over an imaginary child that holds them together from a boarding-school distance. In the all-male production of *Who's Afraid of Virginia Woolf?* it would be hard to believe a child could ever keep two men together.

Who would I marry? I thought about it with J.T. standing there. I thought about it in the sun where I was widening. I was surprised to be thinking about marriage. I'm sexually conservative, but mostly radical in other ways. I didn't think I could ever marry a man again. Officially or not officially. There wasn't a ceremony, per se, to legitimize that first marriage. I was still young enough to feel that any real time away from home was only like running away.

I loved a man named Richard. I told my parents. I moved away from one house into another house. If the family is a cult, the journey out of Brooklyn was leaving the cult for love life. I knew I wasn't going to get the love kit down in Brooklyn. Thomas Woolf said only the dead know Brooklyn.

I'm not much for cults or rituals, but I like the way séances look and feel. The dead rise in a glamour of nostalgia and goofy knowing, all without technique.

A Wedding in the Sky

The mind of the medium is the whole show. Marriage is the séance's opposite. Marriage is too sealed, too poised on the future. Marriage is too much money in the bank. It's strict with the idea of being the right thing. It's a step in logic, rapturous or dreadful. I know two people who got married so they could break up.

Richard and I got married so we could stay glued to the future. We had a strong sense of the future because we were monogamous. We believed in the old idea of romance. We didn't keep a lot of company. We kept money in the kitchen. We stayed off the subculture and out of the pride parades. We weren't proud that we were gay, just happy about it, happy to have met. I met him in the theater district, in a bar, and then the next week I went to see him at the restaurant where he worked. I was sitting at a table and Richard came out with a tablecloth. He threw the tablecloth over my head and starting setting the table on my head. Then I loved him.

I was going to be a dancer, which is what I was doing in the theater district. Studying being a dancer. The jazz dancer, Luigi, said that the source of all movement was the asshole, but I side with Isadora who said it was the solar plexus. I could feel more life in my solar plexus and more tragedy. If the asshole were really the source, I think we would all be doing a dance about getting out of our own way. I was going to be a dancer because I had fallen in love with a dance teacher at Bennington College who made dancing look like living. He had a glamorous habit of dancing into my dreams every night. And so I woke up wanting to dance. Then I woke up in a studio and played a piano for the dancer I loved, and he was dancing to the music I was playing for him.

I wonder if relationships are best measured when they're understood as a variation of the self making enough room for someone else—dancer for the music? It's harder now to accommodate for the physical fact of *him*. I'm on the next level of being free. The space that was so easy to part inside me has been filled in by who I am without him. Something more, again, about myself. But I don't know what it is. Who will I be when I am finished filling in all the inner space? Am I filling it up with absence or consciousness?

Part of Richard's consciousness was taken by a dream about picture taking. He always wanted to be a photographer. I stayed in New York after we broke up and he went to South Carolina. Richard moved into a house with everything photographic crowded in around him. He moved into a bunker based upon career. The house had very low ceilings and reminded me of the chicken coop my great aunt in Long Island had converted for her and a girlfriend to live in a thousand summers ago. Richard's house was dark.

And Pelion, South Carolina, was dark leading into Columbia, South Carolina, and then into the sky. Some of Richard's photographs were of young boys he had met at the university. Gorgeous boys—a glamorous fact that was hard to put alongside the other fact that

Richard had stopped having sex. He told me he had stopped having sex because there would never be someone like me again in his life in the South and how dark it was there now and why bother having sex when there was nobody like me. I told him to get a real life. I told him to go have sex. I told him about how I went and had sex whether it meant anything or not. Life or not. Love or not. I had sex to work the muscle, to open a door made of people. To connect. I told Richard why I had to go and have sex. Then I was alone and Richard was alone, which meant that we couldn't be together.

And because he was celibate, there was something wrong about all the pictures. They were noisy. And sneaky. They were taken by someone leering, someone who had forgotten the body, someone who wanted to steal sex. They were erotic pictures taken by someone who wanted to erase the erotic. I began to think of my ex-lover as someone I didn't know at all. Or was he turning into his anti-self? It was a different self there in South Carolina reflected in the rest of the domestic surroundings. Nothing about Richard, exclusive of our relationship, ever made it into the room, settled on the feel of clean sheets, or added to the toughness of old silk that got pulled taut enough so it could be nailed to the frame of a couch he probably found on the street.

After I left South Carolina, I wasn't in touch with Richard until a few years later. We had one of those phone conversations you might have with an old relative with whom you haven't kept up your end of the bargain nobody signed. You love them, but you've stopped telling them you love them. Or in some cases, you can't remember why you do, apart from the fact of blood. Which isn't love, but the rhythm of someone coming back, leaving, coming back again into the other person's life they don't quite know how to stay put in.

Richard told me that he runs every day, stopped smoking, and still loves me. And still has no sex. He hasn't met the man. I haven't met the man either. And I wonder if my—what still feels like *new*—independence has put me in a country of dreams and actualizations I couldn't possibly inhabit with another person, couldn't ask of another person. I am so fiercely about one life. I can't call one life what I used to call it. I can't call it loneliness anymore. I don't know what to call this thing I have.

The End of Being Known

The sex with my twin brother began in the first lap after puberty. We were living near the park in New York City. I can still see the sun set behind the roofs that lead down to the Hudson River, but I can't see the sex as well. I only remember the quality of it and how now it has become a sort of nuance whenever we get on the phone. Sex has given our life of brothers an intonation. We never judge it or marvel at it or allow it to ruin our lives in any discernable way. We just *sound* this way — like brothers who had sex with each other.

When I call my brother, I feel more comfortable leaving a message on his machine. And whenever I do, I'm disarmed sometimes by the outgoing humor of his messages: "I'm off to the sad opening of a girls' school" or "I've been dragged away to the blessing of the ships" or "Are you sure I know you?" or, better, "Are you sure you know me?" The messages could easily have been written by the famous monologists Ruth Draper or Anna Russell because they have this formal hysterical quality to them. They're funny messages, in other words, but not funny to everyone. They're *acquired* funny, like satire.

47

The messages are particularly not funny to my father, who calls up my brother on the phone occasionally. My brother or me being funny is never funny to my father. My father thinks being funny is something you do when you're not sure about your real purpose in life. Being funny is the summer job. Being funny is extra. But I'm used to my brother's humor. I can see my brother through his humor, no matter what else is happening to him. I can tell what his humor is disclosing or what his humor is obscuring, because my brother is my twin, which makes him differently like me. In that way, nobody sounds like my brother talking into his tape except me. We have the same speaking voice, which wavers somewhere between gravel and gravel and gasoline.

We have become famous for our voices and are known by them more than we're known by our faces or anything psychological, anything under the surface, anything that might throw one off the sound of the voice. We're twins who *sound* alike, not twins who look alike, even if we look alike. Some people have the habit of listening to my voice and not what my voice is saying—loving the music without understanding the lyric. But music can tell you what a lyric means, so some people have this *sense* of me—that it's almost all of me. Me, as my voice. Which can also be intimidating.

Somebody recently said—for the hundredth time of getting told this one thing precisely—that I can be intimidating until you get to know me. But aren't most people? Isn't the human voice always slightly intimidating until it is singing?

I'm sure the gravel and the gasoline come from the early intonation around the language Kevin and I spoke before we learned English. Many twins go through the experience of having the world in their mouths in words only they can understand. It's the way they communicate with each other so they don't have to communicate with anybody else. They strike an early bargain to double private life.

Because twinship begins in narcissism, English can be the thing that breaks the mask—a symbiosis with a dominant but, for the twin, *other* language. A twin joins the world outside his twin world the moment English takes over and the made-up language falls away like a veil between the two dancers. Still, even in English, the twins know that it was that first language that set a tone. They know that the sound they made was filling up the loneliness of being different.

Because I sound like Captain Hook (according to the writer Allan Gurganus), I tried doing voice-overs for a few years but nobody really knew how to cast me. I wasn't a hard seller. I could only sell a voice and not the thing the voice was selling. Whenever I went into an audition, people gasped at my unique sound, but I could never book a job. People didn't know what to do with me. I wasn't marketable. I was too unique. I've always been too unique.

Once I was in a songwriting workshop during the

1970s and ended up being shut out of the big showcase at Reno Sweeney's after the last class because I was too unique. I stood out from my fellow songwriters, which I had thought was the point. Being a twin makes being unique the point. But away from the double, standing out wasn't the point.

Packaging has always been my problem. Nobody knows how to label the box that has me inside it. Because I could never tell exactly what set me apart in the niche sea of voice-over voices, I kept complaining to my agent about not booking work, and she kept telling me it could take five years to really get a career started. It's an audition business—a harried string of appointed times that rules over any actual work. I didn't do a good audition. I wanted people to know I had a famous voice without selling them a famous voice. I don't want to be famous; I want to be loved, unlike a real actor, who switches the love with fame.

The voice-over world is a fantasy world, like every entertainment. All the work is booked by a dozen people who've been in the business since Lauren Bacall, and she was the last of the really unique sounds. Most people, if you listen to them on television selling you the soap or the candy bar, sound pretty much the same. My voice of damage-through-excess isn't popular anymore. I can be ahead of my time, but I'm miserably behind it when it comes to popular culture. I've never made any money from any of my contributions to popular culture. But I'll pay the money it costs to get in, sometimes.

I spent a lot of money on learning voice-overs. I had the best coach, the best agent in New York. Then I couldn't get work. Then somebody said the reason people leave the business is that they run out of money (from all the demo tapes and coaching sessions), which, I suppose, just justifies not making money.

It's a sham in a way, but there were some nice people. I had a nice enough agent. Some of the casting directors were funny—if that's the right word. Sometimes today I'll see a casting director or an agent at a movie. I will be out in the world of no voice-over work, and somebody will say they know *that* voice, they *remember* that voice. I will be in a restaurant or on line for a movie, and someone will say, "Michael, is that you?" as though they can only see me by what they hear—as though they're listening to the voice through a curtain. And only after I've uttered, "Yes, it's me—how are you?" can they put the voice to the face.

It can be tricky on the phone sometimes. When the sex lines were invented I called one, and as soon I started talking, a voice in that sea of chat-room voices cried out, "Klein, is that you?" As soon as I talk, I break my anonymity. People can't *see* me without *hearing* me, which is mostly how I am remembered. And because I am a voice, people don't take the usual photograph of me with their minds. They make a recording.

Like my brother is making a recording. His sound, what he lays down on the outgoing message, is entering the world at large more than it is entering the mind of anyone specific. He doesn't have many people in his life who would call him. There's only me and my father, Roy, most of the time. And sometimes Marie, a half-sister.

My brother isn't a social person anymore. He's trying to stop drinking, so he doesn't go to the bars as much as he used to. He doesn't think very much about knowing people. Sometimes it feels as though my brother thinks that knowing people is a phase that he went through already. I can understand that, in a way. People are a lot to know.

Because he is alone, my brother reads and writes. He freelances. He sees people at the movies. Seeing people is enough of people. He's been hurt by people more than I've been hurt by people. When I look at my brother, he looks back like he's been held up by what hurts him, and so when he's late for something, it's his big-picture pain that makes him late.

There was a story yesterday about a dolphin. The dolphin looked into a mirror for the first time and found himself at exactly the same moment he was alive. As startling as the image was, it also gave the dolphin the feeling that there was more than just one reflection when considering one's self. Self meant he was one among others. I'm a dolphin. Most people are dolphins, I think, especially if they have the capacity to love. My brother can be a dolphin, too, but mostly I think he's fixed in the one gaze he knows will be there—like it was when we only had each other to conquer childhood. We weren't going to make it without each other. There were so many storms my mother and stepfather made outside the room. They were medicated lovers. They weren't going to give us the tools to make any repairs you sometimes have to make in a storm. They didn't have a toolbox that didn't have pills in it.

My parents didn't know how they made it as far as they precisely did make it, so they weren't going to give us that particular experience—the experience of *making it*. They weren't going to give us the American Dream because they didn't go to bed to have it. So, let's say my brother and I had each other because we didn't have our parents. My parents got lost coming home from a dance. Then my brother got lost. Then I got lost. In this way, I'm not my brother's life. I'm at the movies in New York. My brother is at the movies in Boston. We've been at the movies from the beginning, from the beginning of the movie.

There's a coolness at the movies about life. Everyone in the theater shines under the same story in the dark, the smell of popcorn mixed up with the smell of chocolate and perfume. Safe. It meant a lot to us in childhood. Recording moments people were safe. Like what an answering machine does. The person making the message is safe. Safe, in their voice anyway, inside their voice. A voice can live after the person falls away from the voice.

Or a person can only live as long as the voice keeps living. I make up my brother because I got lost. Every fear is a wish. My brother lives in the steel light of a blade. He walks, as if in a dream, toward danger. He improvises with alcohol in a play about an alcoholic who lives in Boston. He keeps a distance. He can't sleep. He thinks there is something going on without him. He is infatuated with the homeless. He smells danger and death when he's drinking. Anything bad can happen to him. By accident. I make my brother up.

My brother is on a street he's lived on for a while, in the neighborhood of the shadows from the lamps in the summer. Everyone knows his name, but no one ever calls him by his name because he's a faggot. They call him faggot because it's the name the world gave him. My brother will die in the world's name for him on a street where someone is killed once a month or so. I make my brother up.

He can't stop living in the bad neighborhoods. I know my brother can afford to live in better places, but he chooses to live close to sudden death. There seem to be more churches there, where they feed the homeless man my brother picks up every few weeks to come live with him—until he can get his shit together he always manages to say when he calls to teach me about the homeless. In the world my brother lives in, the streets give up their homeless. My brother is their king. I make my brother up.

My brother's love suits the men the street gives up to him. He has sex with the homeless man because it's all his heart can afford, what it is already used to, what it has had already—sex with someone who thinks my brother is more powerful. It will not be a homeless man who kills him, finally. It will be a sudden stranger: the addict, the homophobe, the crazed. It will be someone the world has come to name instead of see. My brother doesn't name anything in the world, or he forgets to. And without the naming, my brother doesn't discriminate. He has the ability to get under a person's skin. He makes a wholehearted effort at the beginning of a person in his life to love the person in his life.

The love I have for my brother is different than any other kind of love I have for another person. It's a love with a limit. When it's used up, there won't be any more of it. It's a contract. It's not a love that grows over time, but one that actually diminishes, becomes logical and objective and judgmental in a way I don't like love to be or even thought it could be. I guess it is something other than love. I guess what my brother and I have now is something that happens after love. And something about the love or whatever it is, now that it's had so much life shooting through it, has a force about it that has nothing to do with him, the other one. This . . . whatever it is . . . follows us like a mechanical cloud.

But love won't be staggering up the hill or down the hill or down the street my brother lives on the night he drops the world, the night I make my brother up. My brother would have just closed the bar. Love didn't walk in that night, and he will be almost gone in the vertigo wave of his stagger. And someone will stab him and leave him under the streetlight. The streetlight will be like the end of the movie *West Side Story*, when everything comes down to Bernstein's operatically alone basso ostinato under what's left of the music and the camera suddenly, self-consciously, pulls away from the New York playground. And for the first time in his drunk and sober life, my brother will be amazed that he can hear children on that street because all he has ever heard was the music of craving, and the music of craving doesn't happen to children. The music of craving is not about children. Craving comes from speeding up the heart beyond what it needs to live. Children have all the world they need. They have it, and we want it.

My brother will be amazed that everything has turned out this way. And at the clarity of it. That on that particular day in summer, everything will end with his death pushing into the street and into the sky. And before it ends, he will put his hand over his craving heart, and a line from one of his poems will keep saying itself to him over and over: *the beauty of the broken law, the broken law of beauty*—his imagined life and his un-imagined life talking to each other. My brother will die violently and his last breath will have beautiful language in it. Then a crowd will form, the way it always forms around the new dead thing left by a summer tide or storm with nothing left but a story of how the dead thing left came up. A crowd of strangers will make up my brother's life, the way that I have made up my brother's life.

Let's say, for the story's sake, I know I will get that phone call one day, the one telling me my brother is dead. I will be in bed with a book or will have just no-ticed the semen on my chest run clear, the way it did on his chest a thousand years ago in a bedroom of reck-lessness. Let's say, if I go back a thousand years ago to the bedroom that floats in the time line between two cities, that there's something there and something after leaving there that my brother would never say, could never face. Something to do with our father and our mother and death and booze and aloneness and togeth-erness and sex the first time. Let's say that maybe I'm not in a love relationship with another person because it's too specific. Maybe I'm in love with the world.

I don't see my brother very much today. I *hear* from him, as they say. I see him in my mind, floating above the city shaped like a knife. Or I see him in a dream, arguing. I see him shaking a tree at me from the bottom of a lake. And when I think of it, if he does die first—summer, the street, a stranger's blade of light slicing through the air of a children's playground song—I will not be released. His death will not release me from his life. It will add to him. But what makes me think it—that *my brother will die first?* The murder I am so careful to report, in a minutely detailed fantasy, might happen years after I die myself. Or it could never happen. Or it could happen to me. What is it about my own life that makes me feel compelled to drag the river of my brother and me for a corpse? Who am I, suddenly, in my mid-forties, alone, and inhabited by my brother's future ghost?

I have a better life now that I've stopped drinking and managed to, at least, get off the same road I'm so invested in tracking him down on. But why hasn't this given me empathy for my brother? Why can't I love him when I have been him—been drunk, been in the arms of the homeless man, thinking I was home. Why do I imagine violence rather than a plan to save my brother? I can't save him. I don't know how to save him, even though I've been him. I never saved that part of myself that was him, I just stopped it. When did I stop loving my brother and why?

My mother never dressed us in the same clothes or sent us to the same schools. And she hated the curious women in the grocery stores or public parks, peering into our carriages as though we had just landed from outer space. To those women who asked "Are they twins?" my mother curtly replied, "No, they're chicken pot pies!"

After being pies together, my brother and I did puberty together in a small apartment in Greenwich Village, while my parents argued about money. I turned up the radio whenever my parents argued. Or talked.

"I'll never get married," I said.

We were in a kind of marriage. It was a marriage that brought some strange comfort, but it was the wrong thing to be mastering—like having to get used to eyeglasses at a young age.

The first orgasm I ever had was with my brother. We were twelve, thirteen. We came to sex like hoodlums. We circumvented authority. My brother and I never got the talk about sex or anything about what might happen to us. We never got anything futuristic. My parents didn't *pass down* anything experiential or teach us any real lessons because their own experiences, their childhoods, had been filled with utter dread and anxiety.

I think my parents figured my brother and I would pass everything we had to know between each other and it would be enough. They could give us food, clothing, shelter, stuff, but a lot of thinking about the world and what it could do arose out of the twin consciousness that thrived at night when show music and traffic honked through the Greenwich Village of my youth.

My brother and I talked about the world as though we had landed on it. But maybe my parents landed too. Maybe they were still landing, learning to land. Maybe we *don't* choose our parents.

I touched my brother's body for the first time when we were ten years old and we were alone on a stage in the ballroom of the Pine Orchard Country Club in Branford, Connecticut. We were going to be actors/singers when we grew up, we told each other. We were going to write music and plays. Whole universes would spin away from us into an unsuspecting, but soon-to-be adoring, audience. We were going to be famous for what we *thought*.

In the country club my brother and I choreographed a little number (walking with some kind of elaborated arm movements from downstage's powerful left and right diagonals). We were walking in a slanted way toward each other, humming, "All day, all night, a band of angels watching over me, Oh Lord," or was it, "Ain't she sweet, just a-walking down the street, now I ask you very confidentially, ain't she sweet?" After we got to the front of the stage and finished our song, we kissed each other. On the lips.

Eventually, and for about a year, my brother and I were doing it once or twice a week. He would come to my room, or I would go to his, and one of us would just linger there in the doorway until something like permission arose. We kissed. Again. Then my brother sat to the side of me on the bed and ran his hand slowly down my chest and stomach until it reached a beating cock. He kept his hand on my cock a minute, which was when I'd come out of the temporary coma and start reciprocating. I'd grab my brother by his shoulders and push him down to my mouth, which was dry inside but moist at the lips. And we'd kiss again, the second time. And that would be his cue to start climbing up on me, to stay tethered by his tongue inside my mouth but also to move his legs on either side of my body, so that by now he was straddling me. We didn't know what fucking was, or we would have fucked. And so we were oral lovers. And when we sixty-nined (the last move because by then we were always so close to coming and we both wanted to come in the other one's mouth), I always saw us as the snake we had become, swallowing its own tail. It didn't feel like having sex with another person or even having sex with another boy. It felt like an extension of my own sex.

I knew my brother was another body, another cock, another heart. But we were in puberty together, and we always came together. And in that miniature heartbreak I felt just after orgasm when I went back to seeing him as another person—the assigned brother, as everything other than sexual (someone who got up five minutes later than I did and didn't have friends in school, someone lost in books and classical music)—I was struck with something I might now call regret. Or maybe it was an early moment of knowing what it was like to be alone.

Then I knew that my brother and I shouldn't be doing this. When the year of our sex was drawing to its close, he came to my room and I had to tell him that I didn't want to have sex anymore. It wasn't a decision based on anything except how I felt. I didn't think what we were doing was wrong, but I started to want to break away from my brother, in thinking, in feeling, and to become whoever I was supposed to be without him. I wanted to spend time *feeling alone*. The sex became like an animal we had been feeding, and I wanted to let the animal go.

"We should be having sex with other people, not each other. With girls or something."

"Girls?" (As if I'd said gorillas.)

"Yeah. Don't you like girls?"

"I think about them, but I don't know if I like them."

"Well, maybe you need to think about them longer. Maybe we should try it with girls from now on, like other guys."

"I wouldn't know where to start."

"By talking to them, for starters. There are plenty of girls at school who really like you."

"It's you they like."

"That isn't true. I just talk to them more than you do."

"What if we like boys?"

"I don't think so. It's different when it's us. I mean, I don't think of you as a boy, I think of you as my brother."

My brother was beginning the homosexual dream. But I didn't have the homosexual dream until somebody else could give it to me, someone who wasn't in the family. I didn't have the homosexual dream until Henry from school. Henry stayed over one night, and more nights, until we had sex. Then my brother burst into the room. In the weird breeze made from my brother bursting into the room, I felt the secret of sex with my brother whisper to the sex I was having with Henry. Henry was the homosexual dream I was having because I had stopped having my brother. I had woken up from my brother's dream, the dream of my brother. But my brother was still dreaming; *is my brother still dreaming?*

Later my brother and I came up against what sex was like in the world. We went swimming at the YMCA. The swimming counselor, Larry, walked around the locker room one day with an erection and sat down beside Kevin. He started massaging my brother's shoulders. I was fascinated and unnerved by Larry's moves on my brother. As cool as I might have been about the sexual heat of the relationship that was now over, seeing my brother move into the light of another human being made me queasy.

Larry was attractive—tall and lanky, with a shock of black hair. His eyes were gray and they looked frightened, but that didn't make me think he was afraid. I saw the other thing you sometimes find in another person's eyes: the ability to hurt someone. I told my brother I would meet him outside. I waited for almost an hour. When my brother appeared, he was washed out. He was white as the sun. Then my brother said, "He made me have sex with him."

"Made you?" I said, finding it hard to believe it wasn't consensual. Suddenly, in the real world of negotiation, danger, and despair, sex was currency.

"Yeah, I didn't want to do anything."

"Well, what did he make you do?"

"Suck his dick."

It was the first time I ever heard my brother say the sentence, and it shocked me for a minute before I fell under its spell. Sucking anybody's dick was such a specific. I had heard of having someone by the balls, but having someone by the dick was even more possessive, demonstrative.

Larry asked my brother to come along on a sleepover the swimming group was having the next Saturday in the Catskills and to bring me along. The counselor wanted to have sex with me too. But my brother said no. My brother couldn't hold what happened in his mind long enough to think there could be a future in it. He couldn't hold the sex up to the light or share it with anybody.

Then, the way twins do when one of them is talking, I saw what might have happened. I saw the woods in my mind as though they were my experience. I saw myself with Larry. I saw the campfire, pretending to be asleep, waiting until everyone else was asleep before finding Larry in his sleeping bag or Larry finding me in my sleeping bag. I saw myself unzip Larry's sleeping bag from the bottom and crawl between his legs and just be a head moving up and down in the dark. And then I heard Larry groan and cough, to keep the groaning from the other boys.

I looked Larry up in the phone book but never called him. It was important for me to know where Larry lived, to make him real, I suppose. I wanted to see Larry in broad daylight, with clothes on. And for months, after everything had started dissolving into the forgotten and my brother and I settled back into the more familiar confusions that would have calculable outcomes on the future, I liked to imagine Larry walking down the street on his way to swimming class. And I wondered, too (always closing the curtain on the thoughts of him with this), which boys were treading water in his hungry mind now and how long had they been treading there?

I never told my brother about looking up Larry. It was my secret, the way crushes on some boys *(Milo, Milo)* in those days were secrets. And until recently, I rarely spoke about the sex I had with my brother. We're in our forties now and sometimes when I look at him I can't imagine I ever touched my brother's body. It's hard to explain why I had my brother as my lover for that year, however many years. Those glistening, erotic, ecstatic, and dark fragments of time feel like continents breaking off from each other, indistinguishable in the water, floating away from the populations.

In one scenario I make up for the past, I say that the sex with my brother kept us out of the danger zone. The world could unhinge at the dining room table, when my mother was so drugged up that she more than once fell asleep with a lit cigarette in her hand. But with the sex I had with my brother, the cigarette didn't look so dangerous. There was no guilt or shame, just a rash of self-consciousness that broke out sometimes when secret life happened too close to lived life.

And it's easier now to say I don't love my brother anymore, though I still don't understand it. Nothing about love comes with directions, but I know that I should be there for the other person. For example, I should be there to help with my brother's drinking or trying not to drink. I should go stand next to my brother and feel what it feels like just to stand next to him.

But I can't stand next to my brother. My friend A. said once, "You have to go and stand next to your brother and just feel what it's like to stand next to him." Maybe someday, when I am finished being a different person than my brother is. Today I am a different person than somebody who was in love with his brother. I left my brother to go into my life. And he left me to go into his. Or maybe I've just been dreaming. In my dream, I leave my brother alone on a stage in the theater of our time.

A String of Variances

My father loves my brother because they taste the same. Like alcohol. My father loves my brother because they both skip certain tracks of life. Like the empathy track — they skip that one a lot. There is something else that draws my father toward my brother like a lover, but I don't know what it is. It's a dream draw. I'm in the wake of my father and brother dreaming. My friend R. says that fathers who spent a long time in a war love their sons in a way like they know better than the child knows about what's good for them. My father loves my brother like that.

For example, when my brother was between gigs, my father told him to go join the Air Force. So my brother went to Biloxi, Mississippi, and fell asleep with a cigarette, which set the mattress on fire. He flunked basic training, and they put him on the psychiatric ward. My father and my brother never talk about Biloxi. My father isn't mad about the fire or necessarily happy that my brother hadn't succumbed to it.

My father is between feelings like the needle on a metronome is always in the middle of time. Because my father is between feelings, he is a person no one really knows. My father submerges in his own version of the real. For instance, he can't relate to people who have been saved. In this way, reality to my father has no range or delicacy. There has to be a clear plot, which cheapens reality in a way. If there isn't a clear plot, my father sticks one in. He's a plotter father.

Sometimes I imagine him sitting right in the middle of where plots get made. I see my father in the theater, watching a play about my brother and me, two twin boys he once held when there was only romance in the world. Of course, it's a memory play. Even before the intermission my father keeps going to the lobby to smoke a cigarette or make a phone call to a woman he knows, or loves, or is mad at. He misses important scenes. He never sees the plot develop, deepen, change.

When he gets back to his seat, he makes up what he missed without checking it with the person sitting next to him to see if he's right. My father isn't the kind of person who wants to know the truth if he didn't catch it, if he didn't dream it up first. My father is very adamant about telling you the *real* truth if he thinks you have it wrong.

After I wrote a book and sent it to him to read, my father wrote me a letter saying I had it wrong about him and my mother's divorce. In the book, I said the divorce was over money. My father said the divorce was over something else. Then he didn't tell me what it was. I heard the money story from my mother so I put the money in, which was good even if it wasn't true. I wanted something in the book about money because I knew it would be a mysterious part. Money is mysterious to me.

Then I told my father something I heard Tobias Woolf say once, to help him out of his thinking that I had it wrong about life. I told my father that no one can criticize you for the way you remember something. It's a dream, really, that intangible shred of anything we manage to remember. *Truth is relative* is really just an homage to memory. One thing I really do know is true is that he was in the Air Force. Which is why he gave it to my brother. It was something he knew about already. My father didn't have to use his imagination. Because he is threatened in some ways by the imagination, he never questioned the government. The government was concrete to my father the way it is vague to some people. Then my father took up the Air Force plane and learned languages. As soon as he got the world, he wanted to fly off of it. He trusted getting back. He trusted the government. In the 1950s anyone who didn't trust the government didn't have much moral support.

All that's kaput. Now we know. Too much, my father thinks. We know what we once suspected. That none of it works. The meek actually don't get to inherit the earth. The way my father loves me is the way he loves the real inheritors or a business or the government. He goes on the mission the government gives him, but he doesn't know if he'll come back in one piece.

Still, he goes. It's his job, just through the door of being alive. My father knows I'm there, beyond the door, in his mission. But he doesn't know very much about how I got there, or if he can ever fully meet me there—more life alongside his already life—which makes my father *think* about love more than feel about love. He's a thinker, my father. And a talker father. My father calls from far away to talk to my brother and insults my brother's outgoing message into the incoming message. If only they could overlap. If only my father could interrupt my brother's Draper or my brother's Russell. But he can't. Technology has made it so that he can't overlap or interrupt. My father gets one chance to hear the sound of my brother being out of range. My father's one chance is a variance of: "Hey sonny, get a real life." Or a variance of: "Hey sonny, it's time to get your shit together."

My father is a string of variances, like those thin leaves of see-through color I watch curl away from the heat of spotlights in an auditorium on Eleventh Street, where we are living in New York. We have to interrupt the rehearsal of *Oliver!* so Mr. Kreitzburg can climb the ladder and change the gels. The auditorium is in the wood-lined heart of a school called P.S. 41.

One day, two girls find me in the lunchroom and tell me they have something to show me, etc. I know they are bad girls. They dress like bad girls. They look like Ida Lupino in a prison movie or Gloria Graham or Lizbeth Scott. Their clothes look like rain gear. Or like just rain. I know they have done other things to other classmates. They have done things like twisting arms and challenging other classmates to fights. I can't imagine challenging somebody to a fight. It's like telling somebody they aren't real.

After the stairs and my shirt and pants and underwear and shoes and socks that float through the landings and bump off the red banisters on the way down, real life comes back in the form of a rehearsal. I walk through the auditorium. Naked. I find my costume backstage. I wear a pair of pants that don't make it to the floor of the stage. I wear an old T-shirt. My brother and I are the best actors in the school, which basically means that the teachers love us and the students hate us. I'm playing Oliver and my brother is playing Fagin. Oliver is looking for his mother, for love, for someone to tell him his soul is wider than an orphan soul.

Fagin is looking for money. Actually, Oliver and Fagin are looking for the same thing. Security. But Oliver is the softer role, which feels closer to who I really am. It is the role of a lifetime. It is a role written around wonder and empathy and a certain naiveté about men and women. Fagin is tougher. Fagin is older, bathed in blue. He is the adult looking for the child, and Oliver is the child looking for the adult.

My brother plays Fagin the way I would play Fagin. Cranky, but with a sense of play. My brother and I share an aesthetic already. We like the same things, but we have different spins, different approaches, which my parents think they can see or understand. The way my parents tell us that what they see is the truth is how they break open their version of Christmas. One Christmas my brother got a little sports car you can actually drive around in and I got a puppet theater.

In the play *Oliver!* I improvise, while my brother rests his arm on the banister of knowing his lines—puppet sensibility versus car sensibility. My brother likes to know where he's supposed to be standing by the time he's finished singing a song called "Reviewing the Situation." When I'm finished with the song "Who Will Buy?" I might as well be floating in the clouds. I never remember exactly where I'm supposed to be standing, and I don't think about it, really. But the director doesn't seem to mind. She's transfixed directing twins. She's never worked with twins before. She thinks twins are trick dogs.

Acting feels like something my brother and I are naturally good at, which means we never know how hard it is. We're undisciplined in that way. Inside both my brother and me is something that floats in air—an aesthetic without craft. Inside me are dandelions. I forget if dandelions are the yellow part or the part you blow away.

There's a scene in the play where I've been adopted by an undertaker and don't want to live with him. I escape from his house and have to go through a window into the backstage. In the escape, between leaving the stage and entering what's behind it—the backstage of heavy curtains, cables, painted sets, and the *E-X-I-T* glow—I feel the moment has an indelible aspect to it. There's a life behind my life. Backstage has this excited, surprising feel to it. In *Oliver!* my big songs are "Who Will Buy?" "I'd Do Anything," and "Where is Love?" Love is abstract, but I don't know that yet.

The way I didn't know that Oliver and Fagin were both looking for the same thing. I just know they're in the same play. Like me and my brother. Singing. I think singing will bring people to me. I think I will be discovered singing. I think when they find me dead someday I would have just been singing. My brother gets to sing "Pick a Pocket or Two."

I switch roles with my brother in a dream. We spend our childhood switching roles, switching classes, switching boyfriends and girlfriends. In the dream, I'm Fagin living in a den of beaming male youth. We live in a loft in Brooklyn. I send my graffiti artists out along the rail lines to mark up the city. This isn't Fagin's money dream. There isn't any money anymore. I take the boys from their mothers because I love them more than any woman does. I know what they need. Which isn't just physical. I tell them that my love will turn into money.

In *Oliver!* I make asking for more sound like singing. My brother makes the song "Pick a Pocket or Two" sound like an anthem. A march. We are good little actors. Singers. Troopers. On stage. Off stage. School. On the way home. Home. Life behind life. Electricity backstage. We're discontent. The actor is like the poet in that way. Discontent, no identity. In a letter, Keats said the poet has no identity. The poet is the most unpoetic creature in the world. The poet is anonymous.

I decide later that I will be anonymous. I will join groups without telling other members things that don't have to do with the group directly. I will be part of the group not as *myself* but as a *member* of the group. Nobody will know how I get money. Nobody will know how I move through sex or relationships. And so on. I will get the whole picture in a group. I will get the sense of my own insignificance. My father makes me feel insignificant, so this should be a remembered feeling. But it won't be. This new insignificance will be expansive, while my father made me feel constrictive.

Like he made my mother feel. My mother divorced my father the same year I was singing "Where is Love?" My father shifted his 1962 Triumph convertible into park and put it on a boat headed for Germany because there was nothing left for him in America. I'm guessing there was nothing left. I may be wrong. He may very well have buried a dream somewhere, right under our lives.

In Germany my father started a business, while my brother and I were listening to music and waiting for the dream to end. I didn't understand anything about my father moving to another country, another wife. I didn't understand how he learned German so quickly. But I forget. My father was good at languages. I'm musical but have no sense of translation. Of turning meaning into more meaning. The way I hear it first is the way it is. I have some shame around only having one language. English doesn't have all the words; I know that. I know, when I'm speaking it, that English doesn't have all the words.

My father can speak Vietnamese and Russian. He once told me he was a spy. Or maybe I made that up. I don't think my father was a spy. Not really. I don't think my father could stay interested long enough in a person to be a spy. My brother and I had a language, but we lost it. Rollo May came to study us before we lost it. Rollo May told my parents it was common for twins to have their own language, which made them stop worrying about us. We spoke our own language until we had something to say to my mother and father. But I think what we said was a song. I think we sang before we talked. I wanted somebody to find me singing. I wanted a singing death. I wanted singing to be the way you left this world. "Without a song, the day doesn't end." John Ashbery. My brother and I sang in the dark before there was language. We sang in vitro. We sang until somebody told us to stop. We sang beyond stopping. My brother and I sang "Angels Watching Over Me."

Sometimes instead of birthday cards or phone calls my father sends us photographs of the tranquil Rhine River he is living on. The river is shining in the margin. In one particularly busy photo, there's a flea market going on, and I can see a shirt shining. Green velvet through the trees. It's him, but I can't see my father fully. Most of him is standing behind the third wife. She is beautiful in a hard way—the way the Rhine is beautiful. My father's wife is named Bridget. By the time my brother meets her, she will drink a bottle of pink champagne and make a pass at him while my father is away on business. Bridget will flirt with me, too, but I won't take it. I will be drunk in a way that makes me stuck in the past where my lover is. My longing will drift out the window like a perfume over the Rhine and back to America. The perfume doesn't pick up anything about the present.

I amuse Bridget, mostly. She can only imagine my life when she says she doesn't understand homosexuality. I don't answer in real time. In my mind's list of things to do, I write down Stein, Genet, Baldwin, and Ginsberg. I will lend her my favorite books if she will teach me German. German is a very hard language for me to learn. The way I am with any language. German keeps sinking with a flourish to the bottom of a lake. My mouth can't find its way around German. I can't feel German's teeth. I can't copy German with my mind. I can't tell what the German gay men think of me, the American, when I ask them to speak in English and they tell me they can't. I know they can speak English. They just won't. They won't speak English because they are being asked to speak English. It would be different if English leaked out of them the way it can in a bar.

My brother drinks cognac like my father does. Cognac is the river that runs through our not talking to each other. When I got sober, my brother had been without a drink for about a year. Then, after my year, my brother went out drinking again. It was like my brother and I couldn't be sober at the same time. Or be other things at the same time. Like writing. Yesterday my brother started writing again. I wonder what will happen. I wonder if we can both do something with the world at the same time.

Sometimes my father would leave me at the bar. My father would leave me at the bar in the middle of a deutsche mark that he just gave to the bartender. All the bartenders knew my father because he was such a good tipper. And he was blond. And lived in America once. They all liked him because he had defected. They liked my father because he was funny in their language. He had translated. When my father left me at the bar, I had to get home alone. Which meant taking a cab. Like I said, I'm not good at languages. I had to repronounce the name of my father's street over and over again until the driver could figure out where I was going. I had to vary the sound of the street name ever so slightly until the right key fit in the lock. Click. Home. When I got home, I crawled through the dark and into my room. My room had a long, ultraviolet ceiling unit that hung over the bed like some kind of detector. I put goggles on sometimes and swam along the purple light. I lay in bed for a few minutes for a brief dose of some German inventor's idea about sunlight. It made me feel like a patient in a room. It made me feel cut off from the rest of the hospital. It reminded me of how I was cut off from my family. Which wasn't really a bad feeling. It was too known to be bad. It had left bad and gone to familiar. When I wasn't getting a tan at night, I climbed out the window and sat in the grass. I looked at the Rhine like someone who was from another time. I looked at the Rhine like I was from the Rhine. The lights of Düsseldorf were as bright as stars, like the sky made them, like Düsseldorf fell to earth. I was in a kind of backstage now. I was in the bigger world. It was there, right under his nose, that I made up my father's life.

In the life I made up, my father had to leave America because he couldn't figure out what to do with kids. In the life, my father found his second wife sleeping with another man and threw him out the window. One floor. So he had to leave America. He was on the run over water. My father drove the silver Mercedes now up and down the autobahn looking for work. When he made enough money to send me a ticket to visit him after my mother died, I thought the trip to him would make up for lost time; that I would meet the enigma; that I would love him; that it wouldn't feel as though time could really change two people; that he would have to love me at least as much as my brother now because I was lovable now. I had turned into love. That it wasn't time that happened between me and my father. It was love. All these years. All this seeing him for the first time after all these years, and the watch on his wrist would be a watch of love. What I wanted most was to hear my father's voice again. I hadn't forgotten so much what he looked like but I couldn't remember his voice. Or how he put sentences together. I couldn't remember his mind.

My father's voice gets left inside my phone machine sometimes in the short, breathy messages, like a stalker's. The messages are all in half-voice. Cancer took the other half. Once my father called to wish me a happy birthday and was startled that someone had actually picked up the phone. He was confused into having to finish the song. His mistake. He thought he was calling my brother. The only reason my father will call me, nowadays, is to find the other son. My brother has a phone, but there are long periods when it doesn't ring because he doesn't pay the bill. Because I know the game my father is playing, I tell him I'm tired of having that kind of relationship. I'm tired of having the kind of relationship that involves me having to face the fact that he cares more for my brother than he cares for me. I'm tired of having to know that—of walking up and down the city, the stairs that lead to the sea and away from the sea, the earth—knowing that I will never reach my father's heart. It isn't so much that I need my father to love me. It's too late for that. I've loved already, without having been loved by my father. I made it up. I found a way. I figured it out.

I wrote a letter about three years ago and told my father that I didn't like how I was being used to get to my brother. But my father never answered me. Then last year he called to say he was going to send a letter. That, actually, he owed me a letter. My father keeps thinking that he'll get to say in a letter what he can't tell me over the phone. So he never sends it. Sometimes I see him in a dream in the middle of a tunnel in Central Park. He is huddling over a little fire like homeless men do. I'm an actor in a play, telling my father from the Delacourt Theater stage to send the letter. It's a pseudo-Shakespeare play. My brother always appears toward the end of the dream, riding on a horse through the tunnel, dressed in a wedding dress, galloping past me and our father. I don't know where my mother is exactly, but I feel the pressure of it suddenly. Not knowing where she is exactly. Then like a breeze off the lake near the Bellevedere Castle that rises out of the park like a myth, I feel my mother in the colors of the dream. Like her being, what makes her herself is what the colors are. When I ask my brother who he's getting married to, he says, with the confidence and blind faith of someone getting married, *The world.* And I'm thinking (or do I say this in the dream?), *Do you propose to the world first, or just do it? I do,* you say to the world. *I did,* the world calls back.

"Maybe you can't be in a love relationship because it's too specific; maybe you're in love with the world," a friend used to say. But she's the only one who knows if it's true.

Once, My Brother

Once my brother was in a hospital. He walked around in a paper crown after the nervous breakdown. The crown was made by a group of fellow crazies who gave it to him because he used to let them circle around his bed at night and jerk off on him. The dirty light in the public ward made my brother look old. I didn't have a lot of family around at that point to go with me to visit him in the hospital. I was relegated to going with a cousin of my stepfather's, who was at least as crazy as my brother was. Her name was Miriam, and she took medication, the residue of which painted the corners of her mouth with white powder. Toothpaste or drug? I never knew for sure. I was going to the crazy house with a crazy person.

When we got to the visiting room, my brother didn't say very much. He riffled through a cigar box filled with little notes to himself. All we could do was listen to him, like the grass. He was delusional: "You know, our father is from outer space. Before I got here, I was sitting in front of a computer on Wall Street when I was working for a bank, and it came over the screen suddenly—in the middle of punching in all this useless information—that Freddy boy, dear old Dad, was sent from space to impregnate our mother. Hence us; hence twins. We wouldn't be twins if Freddy was from this fuckin' planet!"

My brother said our mother was a crow. That she had to turn into a crow in order to have sex with our father. My brother didn't know she was dead. That she had died two weeks before in the middle of my brother's falling. That she had found out everything about being alive and didn't want to know anything more about it. I didn't tell my brother that our mother was dead. Telling my brother would have—what? Sent him somewhere inside himself he couldn't get out of, plunged him through a hole in the ice he couldn't relocate after being carried downstream. Or sent him like an arrow the other way, into space maybe, back to the home planet he found so conveniently on a computer screen.

My father came over to the States and said something to the doctor to get my brother out of there. What could he have said? *Well, Doctor, I am the boy's father* doesn't exactly cover it. My father took responsibility, which looked official in the dirty light. My father said something else to the doctor, something to my brother, something to the doctor again. The picture of my father loving my brother, saving my brother, seems even more public than it was. From where I am, it looks like a transaction in a bank. My brother went to live in upstate New York after the hospital. He got a job in a hardware store and started living in a room with a bed on the diagonal. He began a long-term writing correspondence with a famous composer and wrote to poets to tell them whether he liked their latest book or not.

Before my brother found the store, I let him live with me for a while. Big mistake. I was in my own kind of falling. My falling was unmade of hallucination, the way my brother's was, and made out of detachment. The man left me and I began searching for other men I didn't know into the bushes of Central Park. I had sex in the dark breezes of Central Park. I'm someone else when I have sex in public. I think more about the other person stepping out from the leafy crowd than I do about getting caught. I think the stranger's desire for me is as strong as my desire for him because of the breezes between us, which carry hope into the unknown. Being in public makes it *famous* sex. I came home one night with a stranger from the park and my brother stormed into my room while I was sleeping. He screamed into my face, "You're the devil. You're the devil." I told him to leave. He stormed down the stairs and left the building after shattering the plate glass in the front door and becoming the ex-mental patient, without a place to live. My brother had become the kind of New Yorker that has always lived here, but one that nobody knows. The kind of person (the future will make this happen more often) who pushes people in front of trains because they hear a voice that tells them to do that.

Fugue Life

It happened sporadically at first. There would be a girl that my brother would have feelings for. Or that I would have feelings for. Or that he would have feelings for first, then me. Or me, then him—the girl caught in the limbo Kevin and I made.

One of us would bring a girl home and make out with her as far as our body would let us—i.e., whatever didn't involve *real* sex. The penis, for me anyway, was still personal. It belonged to me. Nobody had ever seen it except the family. My penis hadn't tried to make a journey to the heart of another person through the tunnel leading into them.

I guess Kevin and I came to sex slowly or cautiously—I can't remember the feeling—but I know that we didn't launch into it. We didn't think it was very important. We thought sex was something that would happen to us—whenever—like a job we would get without being interviewed. And almost innately, I think we figured it would happen between us first.

We brought girls home to change the weight of the air of home, which was usually dark and confusing with arguments that were taking place, or about to take place. We brought girls home from the schools when the early darkness carried us back to my mother. But sex and girls were in a country different from most of daily life. And Kevin and I didn't watch the other boys make circles around the girls. We didn't go to the dances. The girls we brought home felt sudden and were even surprised themselves whenever Kevin and I related to them in any kind of sexual way. *Scoring* with a girl meant being able to read her mind.

My first girlfriend, Sarah, lived a block away with her mother, who was dying of scleroderma—a disease so strange and relatively unknown (its victims turn to stone) that whenever I went to her apartment, we would stand frozen in the hallway and sort of drift, finally, into the bedroom where her mother was lying helpless. Sarah's mother was always between us physically or mentally, and so we never really got to know each other in a way that made it seem the relationship could ever grow out of its own soil and blossom.

I liked Sarah and even liked kissing her. But there was something in those beginning days of sex that felt like a rehearsal for—what? A play in which I kept forgetting my lines. Sex was a kind of haphazard performance—a use for the body that seemed to freeze it in time and move a mind sideways, never straight ahead. In other words, sex didn't really get me anywhere. It just measured the body in time.

Of course, none of this seemed true later. Sex would become a thrilling series of connections and disconnections, nostalgic and futuristic. But back then, back in the drifty house I lived in before sex attached itself to my penis or tongue, or my thighs, or my feet and arms and buzzed in my ear—before sex attached itself to my hands and their ability and inability to open and close, before sex finished its delicate thread of power and beauty and, later, *found* power and beauty—it was slow and methodical. Like death.

One summer Kevin went to a yoga camp (*whatever that is,* I remember thinking). I don't know what I did instead that summer, but yoga wouldn't have me. I didn't require the body *and* the mind at once. The only vapor from such a practice that I was willing to inhale was *Autobiography of a Yogi* by Paramahansa Yoga-nanda, which, for some inexplicable reason, had a big effect on me.

Kevin and I had started writing songs at around this time, and aside from our own music vibrating inside our heads (we would never learn to actually *read* notes), we had always memorized each other's songs. I had written one very strange, surrealistic little piece that had a beautiful melody and began with a typically cryptic lyric: "I woke too early this morning, saw the sun before it was born." Kevin liked the song and used to play it for his fellow yoga campers. By the end of that summer, the whole camp was humming this strange little tune, which cheered me.

Years later, I will notice, at the gym particularly, in the showers, that if a man starts humming or whistling, someone else will invariably start replying in kind—a conversation of notes without anybody ever reaching for a word of word-language.

At Camp Yoga my brother met a girl and fell in love for the first time. Roberta Berman was from an affluent family outside Philadelphia, and she smoked pot every day. In retrospect, the drug may have been a more powerful glue in their relationship than either one of them would have admitted then, but it didn't matter. There was a deep bond between Roberta and Kevin, so of course, I was very eager to meet her.

I didn't like Roberta at first. I didn't find her particularly attractive, and she was aggressive in a way that made my impression harden. I was attracted to very feminine girls then, when I started following them into the world of deep feelings, and I don't know why that was, exactly, since now, being queer and the rest of it, I'm much more attracted to brilliant, aggressive women.

Roberta and I eventually did become friends. There was something about her that wasn't like anyone else I had ever met. She was spontaneous and incredibly free in a way that seemed spiritual, at first, but was actually more about her parents' money, which they had plenty of and lavished quite a bit on her. But she did listen to music a lot—which dropped her in another category of freedom, and she heard it, I like to think, the way we all did then, when listening to music was something you actually did as a practice and didn't just turn on while you were busy with something *else*. I remember sitting in the chalk dust of a late afternoon at the High School of Music and Art, listening to Bach's *The Art of Fugue* and thinking, *I'm learning how to hear music.* Since then, it's been a fugue life.

I don't know how it happened exactly—that I grew closer to Roberta and Kevin pulled away from her, but it was a two-year period of reassigning. In the beginning, fresh from yoga camp and playing songs we had both written, Kevin used to take a train to Philadelphia to spend time with Roberta. Then one weekend, Kevin stopped going—I can't remember exactly why—and I started to make the trip.

I don't think Kevin ever had sex with Roberta, and as far as I knew then, I wasn't sexually attracted to her. But I wanted to be near her, and with each successive trip to her parents' home, I was becoming more and more interested in how she lived her life. I liked who I was with her and didn't try and figure it out or talk it over with Kevin or my parents. The whole thing felt like a trance I was in—a trance that, once it hit the part of my consciousness that made me act, simply meant buying a ticket to get on a train bound for Philadelphia.

On one of those visits, something so strange and mysterious happened to Roberta and me that I still don't know how to talk about it. It was as though we had found a way to communicate through thought and feeling only—the way some books will tell you it will be when the Martians come.

Here's what happened: There was a hill near
Roberta's house that, if you stood on the top of it and
moved back a few paces, looked to anyone standing at
the bottom as if you had disappeared. Of course, the
person on the top—Roberta had climbed to the top—
only moved a step down the back of the hill. But somehow, Roberta could see me at the same time that I
couldn't see her—like what happens with a two-way
mirror. The hill let the person on the top penetrate
through it and see the person on the bottom. I couldn't
understand the physical explanation for it, and the
shifting sense of it seemed almost logical if I saw the
hill and its trick as a kind of cadence.

And at that moment of being seen by Roberta but
not being able to see her, I was filled with a regret and
longing so palpable and sudden that I could hardly
breathe. In that moment of disappearance, I was suddenly made aware of feelings I had for her that couldn't
or wouldn't surface any other way.

That night after she left the hill and we walked
home in the dark suburban outskirts of her home,
after something happened that had nothing to do with
us and everything to do with us, she came into my
bedroom, where we kissed for the first time. We never
moved beyond the kiss that whole year. And strange as
it may have seemed to her, there was something exactly
right about it. The hill provided us both the long-
lasting effect of being known to each other in the exact
lapse of not being known. I came back from that

weekend unable to shake the experience of seeing Roberta disappear—a cadence that replaced Roberta and
Kevin with Roberta and me, a cadence that felt so id-
iosyncratic that Kevin couldn't have known about such
things. It had been my moment, in every dimension.

But, oh, I was off about my brother. The first thing
Kevin said to me as soon as I walked through the door
was, "Did she take you to that hill?"

Anonymous Life

The summer I turned eighteen, I lived with a dancer on Mercer Street who didn't know if she wanted to be with men, women, or anyone at all. I had gone through a period of wanting to be with everyone, but at the loft I began the stage of only wanting men. While there had been bisexuality once, I knew it was a multiple that would never add up. Having both sexes was like looking at an eclipse, and in its afterwards, only men were standing in the change—city-bound or sun-drenched at the gay resort. Every solar eclipse seems to refresh an idea you had about the world, and my idea was men and the bodies of men.

The loft where I lived was near First Street and First Avenue, and I used to wander into the Club Baths two or three nights a week to meet male strangers for sex. I liked sex but not social ambition very much, so I didn't go out of my way to meet many people in daylight. Not meeting people paralleled driving a cab all night and that specific kind of loneliness that comes from being in a car.

The undertow of any metropolis is its sweeping loneliness, and New York City lays itself at one's feet with such speed and idiosyncrasy and determination that people feel even lonelier in it. Whenever the odd fare piled into the backseat and lit up a joint, I smoked it with them to ride out the lost feeling. Getting high was popular, like sex, and because AIDS hadn't changed anything yet, sex was still as improvisational as jazz. And like the clubs for jazz, there were clubs for sex too. It was the best time in history to be a gay man, and the Club Baths was the best bathhouse in New York at the time—reimagined some years later as Lucky Chang's famous drag restaurant. Today every table at Lucky Chang's has the ghost of a blow job hovering over it, and the walk-in freezer in the basement still has the pipe in the wall that used to shoot blankets of steam into a tiled room until dawn. The Club also boasted an atrium with a fountain in the middle that lazily arched out its stream of water like spit from the mouth of Puck, and along with an automated snack bar that sold Drake's Cakes, there was a machine that sputtered out coffee through a metal tube, which made it taste like ashes and hot water. But nobody came to the baths for the ambiance. Or the food and drink. People came for the other men in various degrees of disarray or disassociation. And while my aim eventually settled on them—the strangers—I also marveled at the bathhouse staff: guardians of a collective desire whose job descriptions were succinct, the way they are in dreams. One of the jobs at the baths was taking money or refusing money—refusing money from people who were too drunk or crazy; refusing me because I was too drunk or crazy, a lot.

All the jobs at the baths circled around sex but weren't sex. People liked to fantasize that everyone, including the staff, was having sex, but it wasn't true. Sex was for the paying customer and bloomed from the interior—inside the bathhouse rooms, which were flimsy, closet-sized suites, each with a cot up against the wall with a rumpled sheet thrown over it.

Rooms are private, And here we were being private in public, so the sex got poured out of the rooms. We let sex out into the steam of the steam room or the dry heat of the sauna. In the steam room, the heat was blasting out in dream time. The steam was transforming against your skin into a beaded cloak of sexual moisture. You followed someone into a room, without talking—without talking because whatever conversations happened always sounded ridiculous. It was a quiet thing, the bathhouse. It was a museum for sex. And like a museum, you walked around the hallways in a kind of trance. You were on the great desire tour. Your temperature changed with your taste. You had many choices. You fell in love twice in the time it took between orgasms. You flipped between being the pursuer and being the pursued, so that every Eros-syncopated stagger had the same jazziness to it whether you were looking for a man or a dry towel.

One night I was looking for a man or a dry towel. I always found the towel, and sometimes I found the man between the walk and the towel—the one who struggled or didn't struggle past the stricture of anonymity into a conversation or a gesture tinged with desire but also no desire, something approaching how he wanted to be known.

Even at its most relaxed, anonymous sex is anxiety ridden. Because it rows against real intimacy, real sense of taking time, real focus on something other than the body parts and the orgasm (and never its aftermath, by the way—never the cigarette or the telling of a dream), its full sweep of motion is a collapsed moment. You are thinking it is a connection, when really it is a house of cards—a house where all the electricity has gone out, where connections with the person fall toward the center of the initial attraction and can't get back up. The person who participates in anonymous sex does so in order to contribute to abridged sex, abbreviated sex, sex without frontiers.

Edmund White, in his first novel, *A Boy's Own Story,* talks about how much the "sexuals," as he calls them, are in power in our culture. This book was written many years ago, and that's still true. Sex sells, and now sex kills. The anonymous sex partner rarely kisses—like the job-descripted prostitute—and the reason for his being physical isn't as much about fulfilling a desire as it is about changing desire's fluid rhythm with a kind of stasis. A *going dead.* Sex as function.

The anonymous partner generally acts *one* way—there to fuck, get blown, whatever—and feels confused when the stranger leads him, guides him perhaps, into a territory that potentially interrupts the heart—a free-floating desire to suddenly up the stakes and take the chance encounter into a realm of something to be remembered and . . . adored?

One night I met a photographer who came off that night's drug or drunk reliably enough so that I could take him out of there. We fell in love or something. We took each other home a lot. He lived above a seafood joint on Third Avenue, and I thought we were taking each other into the romance of our lives. But my friend *lived* in the anonymous world when he wasn't at home, which was a world I only thought I was visiting. The anonymous world only had sex happening in it, and if it weren't for the sex, I wouldn't have lived in it.

My friend was a trickster. What was tricky about my friend was his hold on real intimacy. It was tentative, like a grip on a banister coming loose from a wall. My friend didn't let intimacy make history. When we fucked in his bed or my bed or dinners or the movies, he wanted to drift back into the old space inhabited by nonconsideration and noncontribution. He wanted to unknow me after knowing me. But really, I told him, it was too late to be anonymous. He knew me already. I worked very hard at him knowing me until he really knew me. So he had to know me. But then he didn't want to know me, and I didn't know why. He didn't consider how time had turned into something close between us, into language and something underneath language that was keeping it going.

Then my friend didn't want language, so I decided to stop seeing him because he wouldn't get beyond the limited idea of whatever it was he thought men did together. Falling in love, according to my friend, was a touchy-feely form of dependency. Homosexuality had given him the homo—a prefix for who he was—but he didn't know if there was enough love that could last beyond the suffix. He thought two men would never have to depend on each other if they were having sex. Having sex would keep them apart, keep them in a performance. Two men could have sex, sure, but fall in love? And so my friend became a stranger who lit a fuse, the staunch independent who combated romance, the narcissist who couldn't merge. My friend only wanted anonymous sex. And so did I, in a way, by having sex with him.

Then, after this, I met a man who became a reciprocal lover, and I began to end not being known. We made some form of intimacy with language in it, until we broke up. We broke up because booze had always been there, holding us too together. After we broke up, I broke off from the booze. And when I broke off from the booze, I didn't want to go back to my lover to try him again. My lover had been the apparition of love the booze made. I wasn't expecting to lose my drug of choice and lover at the same time. A cleaner stream of life started to trickle into what was left of my reckless life. I couldn't support very much yet. I couldn't support old love.

I was single, free. I was an adjective, but not a verb. I acted the opposite of free. I was so serious about staying sober I didn't have any fun. I never went out. I didn't know exactly who I wanted to be. I didn't know how to get through a day, much less a life. There was a long period when I couldn't have sex, even with strangers. I didn't feel like sex. I didn't feel sexy. I felt erotically broke. I felt like having friends more than sex partners because I had no friends in the transition between the booze and the not booze. All my friends had died or were deliberately pushed by me under a wave of alcohol.

Pushing people under a wave made me look awful. So I looked awful when I landed headfirst on recovery's doorstep. Worse even than when I was drinking. When I was drinking I spent money on booze, not food, so I was thin, like a hustler. Getting sober changed my body. I had to eat, but I didn't know what I liked. So I ate everything. I gained weight and let my hair grow. I didn't know how to look. I couldn't remember a time that I ever liked the way I looked—except in an old photograph with a dog. I didn't know what colors looked good on me. I didn't know what kind of shoes I liked or what kind of shampoo. I'd spent many years running from the reflective world. When I was drunk,

I shaved by feel or by candlelight. I couldn't bear my coarse self looking back at me, expecting me to know why.

Then I moved to Provincetown in 1990. I started exercising and living in the sun. I started listening to what men were saying. Listening to men gave me enough energy to become interested in sex again. And so I went back to sex. With a doctor, it turned out. He was a good doctor. Famous. He saw me perform in drag one night in a mess of a play written by a famous French Canadian. The doctor became smitten with me, which, in its gushing, schoolboy accuracy, was the only way I could have been reached by anyone at the time. Courtship, and its affair with the fullness of time, was far too shapeless an engagement.

I did the play because I was free. Free was the feeling that many people have when they reach Provincetown. A frontier of sand and light and driftwood makes everyone a pioneer. And all of it—or a response to all of it—made me an actor. I wasn't a bad actor, but I wasn't a very good one either. I was, however, a natural. I could expand beyond a play's compression of time. In the play I played a transvestite who was insanely fucked up about religion. I had to shave my whole body every other day so I would not appear hirsute, which I was in my nontheatrical life. Because I lost the film of hair between me and water, showers became surreal experiences. The closeness it had to my new skin made it feel like I was bleeding from a place I couldn't see and in a way that wouldn't stop.

Alas, I never got the hang of drag. It didn't reveal the secret, dream me. I drank too much water an hour or so before I went on stage and before my first entrance I had to undo all the femininity keeping me in character to take a piss. The play was being performed at the Provincetown Inn, which was a cavernous, bigger, and flattened-out version of Bates Motel. The inn was perched at the edge of the ocean, and the closest bathroom was accessible only by walking across the stage. And because I couldn't walk across the stage in full costume, I stood outside each dusk and pissed into the breakwater—which, if you haven't tried it, is, most times, like pissing into the wind.

I was attracted more to the doctor's mind, but decided to break my sex fast with him because I knew it wouldn't be melodramatic. Sex with someone you aren't magnetic about is almost more romantic. The body *ruminates* more than titillates. I was still shaking from early sobriety and I was vulnerable. I was accessible. I was listed. It wasn't easy to invent anybody someone could actually like. I felt complex when I was alone, not relieved. I couldn't remember what people liked about other people. The doctor liked me without me coming up with anything. He wasn't demanding about my time or the nature of my character. He knew I was brash and unpredictable and didn't try to get on and ride those qualities.

We didn't feel like we were dating. We were patient. And somewhere under my blonde tumbleweed of hair, he found someone who could make him laugh a lot, but tenuously at first, as though laughter was something he suddenly remembered about being alive. It was great to get so much attention from someone who was funny and smart and successful. I was in something: a relationship, an affair, a comeback. I was in something that was giving me *ideas*. I hadn't had very many ideas for a long time that didn't turn into some sort of trouble. The doctor had ideas, too, but the one about him and me didn't last the season. Then he told me he had a boyfriend in Chicago. We stopped seeing each other as soon as the play stopped running. I had been in two productions at once. On my last night performing at the Provincetown Inn, the doctor sent a bouquet of birds of paradise with a note that said, "Continue to make people happy."

I moved back to New York in 1994. Provincetown was indelible and I would go back there, but it was too small too. The doctor and the acting bug flew out of me at the same time. I continued to make people happy by going back to an old kind of behavior, which meant that the anonymous version of sex found its way back into my bloodstream. But not in the bathhouse this time—this time through the musky and clanging world of the gym. The change in locale didn't alter my behavior. But it was harder to score at the gym in gay steam because it got infiltrated now and then by the wandering heterosexual.

My friends are confused by my continuing adventures in sex. They can't understand why I'm not in the kind of relationship I deserve. Everybody knows what I deserve except me. I tell my friends that I don't go to meet men in bars or clubs anymore because I can't stand waiting on my feet for affection. I don't want to wait for the valet to bring the car around. I tell my friends that anonymity is one resort as long as I play it safe. Then there's a moment with my friends, between the explanation and their compassion, when I see a light go off in their eyes. They know I practice something they'll probably never become as good at as I am. How did I get so good at being anonymous?

Simone Weil in "The Love of God and Affliction": "Affliction is essentially a destruction of personality, a lapse into anonymity." Sex itself had been the affliction. And the fall of blossoms from incest and love unreciprocated—the *little death* of sex—created not a physical but a spiritual vacuum. I love men, but I don't like them as much as I love them—the contemporary dilemma of so many gay men I know. Is there a way for a gay man to honor gay men instead of use them up during sex?

I went to find out. I spent three hundred dollars for some sexual healing. I went to a loft and stood with twenty-nine gay men in Tribeca, imagining what they looked like naked. We weren't embarking on a twenty-hour orgy. We were in a workshop centered on body awareness. Deep breathing. Erotic touch. It sounded retro. It sounded stupid. But it was smart. I was surprised it was smart. I was surprised that people could be articulate about sex. I didn't know sex could sound like this until I heard sex sound like this.

I let myself be a member of the group. I let myself get naked and still be a member of the group. I had known about the workshop for a long time but was afraid of it. Somebody told me the workshop started because of AIDS. It was a workshop to go learn about safe sex. I first heard about it when I was part of a men's group that had gay artists in it. One of the members wanted to turn the group into something similar to the workshop. Something naked. He had been to the workshop and wanted to try it out in our group.

I admired my friend's ambition around wanting to have a new sex story, but I didn't want his story. Not in this room. We were vulnerable enough without being naked. We were wounded. I didn't want to see us *being* wounded. We were a painter, two composers, an actor, and a vocal coach, and we were there to talk about our lives as artists, not as pleasure centers. That's what the workshop was for. The workshop in the loft was centered on talking about and then being pleasure centers. The sexual history of my life didn't seem like it would be directed to this room. The sexual history of my life seemed like it would lead to therapy or celibacy. The sexual history had fires going out and the unlikely match of no booze and sex and not getting naked for a man.

In the workshop we didn't get naked right away. We formed an inner circle and an outer circle. We checked our eyes out. We looked at each other kindly but without giving anything away. The point was to be unself-conscious. The point was to let our selves have an experience without reading the experience through a transparency of the past. Like every class in a New Age school, the point was to be here, now. To breathe.

We breathed on each other. One man laughed a lot. One man scowled. Later I found out that the man who scowled was taking the workshop for a second time. I guess he didn't get it the first time. I guess he didn't feel touched, although he must have been touched. Everybody gets touched here. The glamorous and the not glamorous get touched here. There's a man who weighs 450 pounds getting touched here. I think he is so brave. He is an orthodox Jew. I think he is brave because he tells everybody he came here because he didn't own his cock. His sister and his brother and his father owned his cock. That was a long time ago, and still he is brave.

Before we were naked I got very attracted to one man. I zeroed in on one man the moment I walked into the room, the way it is at a bar or at a party. When it comes to men, I enter the social world to find only one representative. The room filled up with the man I got attracted to. I went over to him and waited until he said something. He had the look of someone who talks first, the look of someone who didn't feel listened to: happy/sad. He did massage. He lived in Queens. He said that Carl Jung had a theory about genius. The pull of the man's gaze made me feel like I was falling inside him, until I hit the Army stint he did in Frankfurt, Germany. Germany was a connection.

I told him where I lived. I told him I was going to write about this but not what I was going to say about this. I didn't tell him how he made me think. I don't tell men what I think of them when they are the new thinking. The man and I make plans to have lunch together. We haven't seen each other naked yet. I imagine that his body is actually more defined than what I can tell through his clothes. His clothes are loose, but not like he's hiding his body. His clothes are loose in that way that makes you think the person is secretly dancing. I tell him that I'm at the workshop so I can feel my body in one piece. He's there, he says, for the massage part.

After lunch we're broken up into groups of four and told to help each member off with his clothes. My team undresses me. I'm overweight. I should have an erection. After the whole group is naked we see each other for the first time. We bathe in the afternoon sunlight of why we're here. It's a consciousness now, a startlingly diverse group. Young. Old. Gorgeous. Not so gorgeous. Self-conscious. Proud. Tentative. The diversity falls away. It begs off, a little. There's something wounded-looking about being naked, something prehistory about it too.

Our next task is difficult for me to enjoy. I have to put on a blindfold. I have to give myself pleasure. I don't feel comfortable in a blindfold. When I am wearing a blindfold I am standing before the firing squad. Isn't that where blindfolds come from? Standing in front of death so you can't see it? I don't want to stand in front of death. I don't owe death anything. When I am wearing a blindfold in the workshop context, I have no one to look at. I can't get turned on. No one brings me desire. I don't know what to do with my cock.

In the workshop we got a list of names for things to do with our cocks. The names were *fire, rock around the clock,* and *juicer.* It's masturbating without intention—cock message without the strict up and down. Each name implies a softer grip *around* masturbation and the idea of pleasure. It's not about the orgasm. The cock is more than the orgasm. The cock is a consciousness. Retro. Stupid. Smart. Then somebody calls the cock a generator. But my generator isn't willing. There's not enough electricity to keep it going. I can't achieve a lasting erection. I can't get used to the lubricant, which is coconut oil but feels more like olive oil or motor oil. We had talked about lubricant earlier in the day. I thought we had decided on lubricant. I thought lubricant was going to feel like something else. I thought it was going to feel personal.

Now I'm taking short and rapid breaths. I echo the beats of a hand drum one of the four assistants is hitting on. I am invited to ask a man to play with my nipples and genitals. I'm mildly erect, but I don't feel connected to myself as much as I do to the effort to connect with him. I want to touch him while he's touching me, but I can't. Or I don't. It's not in the script. There is no script. The sex light is turned on low. No one attacks. No one bites. We are mild. We are sexual the way milk is sexual, or roses. I think my mildness will be read as rejection, but it isn't. After he touches me, he breathes the way I've been breathing. It's the sexiest thing that happens.

The attraction factor looms large in the sex loft. And then you don't act on it. Attraction was what you did before you came here. Retro. Stupid. Smart. In the sex loft, you are on your way to a dance, many dances. One dance might be with a man you don't want to dance with, that kind of thing. My body is reassembling into one piece. I am lying on a massage table for an hour's worth of one man massaging my cock and balls and another man, everything else. I'm tingling. I'm cold. I'm feverish. I'm numb. I am not thinking about sex. I am thinking about dying. I sense living and dying as something that happens at the same time. A line of Beckett rushes into me: "The day you die is just like any other day except it's shorter."

People I know, ghosts, cyclones of light, come and go like fast trains through a lush and heavenly landscape. I connect this energy with the same energy it takes to die. How can I consciously know this?

So this is an event about the ecstatic.

I am convulsively weeping. A lot of us are weeping. In those moments just before the *big draw* (an orgasm of the body, without ejaculation), the whole room sounds like the locked ward at Gay Elsewhere. We are somewhere else, but we have arrived there together. It's time to help somebody else into his big draw. He has a beautiful body. He has a beautiful cock, whatever that is. Was. I get aroused in giving pleasure to someone else. I start to take one hand off his body so I could put it on my body. My massage partner shakes his head. This is about the man on the table. I've had my pleasure.

We wrap a sheet around the big drawer. We invite him to lie on his side. He looks like a baby on a delivery table. Like Billy as he lay dying of leukemia in a Boston hospital. The moment after we watched Billy go into his death, the energy in the room became palpable. I thought the energy was his soul taking its last breath in this world before letting it out in the next.

Do we make love the way we die?

The facilitator of the workshop is asking someone to come take the cock chiseled out of marble, the peace pipe. We're in the circle. We have to talk about what happened to us. We have to put the big draw into a context. We have to have changed. I wanted to fall in love, but I don't say that. Love is outside the box. I say something about the erotic body, just the body. I talk about just the body as it talks to just the other body. My head is resting on the thigh of the man I wanted to fall in love with. We're all like that now in the room, standing on some kind of ledge between love and the body.

That was in November.

Then in August of the following year, I didn't feel as good about the sex workshop as I did when it was happening. The best part for me, anyway, was feeling the death, not the sex. Adding drumbeats and blindfolds to what are essentially anonymous sexual encounters—albeit without orgasm—don't transform anonymity into identity. You just feel less lost because you have a tour guide. You are, in a sense, being authenticated for a behavior that you had, at best, mixed feelings about.

And what are those feelings anyway? That pleasure derives out of an unrelenting focus on the cock? I can understand, intellectually anyway, taking an orgasm through the whole body. But like my breathing with a man was the sexiest thing, the sexiest thing about sex isn't about finding it in its assigned location but where most people forget to look for it—the eyes, the pair of eyeglasses, the accent, the laugh, the limp, the unmistakable cadence of his sentences.

As far as the physical connection goes, I'm back to my own beginning, in a sense. I'm a sexual healing workshop drop-in who didn't really take his big draw into the big picture. The big question I had before the workshop is the same question I have after the workshop.

Why do so many of us feel safer touching men we don't know?

A Resort for the Betrayed

I see a lot of my childhood through water. Three pools. In one pool, I am setting the woods on fire with my twin brother. In another, I am watching my mother's hair undulate into an island of dark smoke. And in the third pool, I am having sex with my stepfather—a shadow whose contours brighten around the continuous, because I instigate the sex to keep him from beating the shit out of me. In this way, the sex has such a timeless quality to it that the verdict of taboo never holds up because the role of seducer falls on me. This is before I know that the one with less experience can never accurately seduce. I couldn't accurately seduce.

When I think about the incest, I recount it with a kind of matter-of-factness and a strange lack of emotional resonance whenever I'm verbal. I somehow forget that the whole affair might seem unreal, disturbing, or even shocking to somebody. Our own stories are the ones that are most mysterious to us, and rather than be trampled by dark evidence or dragged down into an ocean of the past, I speak about my stepfather with a kind of learned ambivalence. I want the brutal facts around the sex to bear the mystery away. I want the story to have an *overall* effect, like it is someone else's story. And it is someone else's story. Incest. Someone else rises out of its ashes. You, but the altered you, still living, but in an abbreviated world. In my heart and mind, I want to live in the worlds the Buddhists call Humanity and Heaven, but I often find myself prowling in the lower worlds of Hunger and Animality, where I've seen a lot of other men prowling too.

It's been many years since my stepfather, and I still think about it, even though he's been dead for almost as long as I ever knew him. I still think about when I used to meet my stepfather in my parents' bathroom in Brooklyn and take his cock in my mouth while he leaned up against the sink and looked down at me until his orgasm made him throw his head away, as if he or both of us were being suddenly forced to taste the confusion of what we were doing.

I still think about how having sex with my stepfather had to fit into a kind of lock, into a certain hour between early and late—the house wrapped in sleep or near sleep—and how my mother slept for years against knowing who her husband and son really were. In a poem called "A Stepfather, a Child," I called my mother's life a "skilled wish rising out of Brooklyn," but the line is an upside down version of the truth. My mother lived in the more desperate affirmative of the wish. All her strength was gripped around the rope of *something wasn't true*.

But she knew what was happening to time. By the look in my mother's eyes, I could tell that she knew I was sucking her husband's cock. I could tell that she knew, by the way she looked down at a book or a magazine in a hard spell of wanting to be taken away by Elizabeth Taylor's latest marriage or Jayne Mansfield's dead dog, that I made excuses to be alone with my stepfather so I could suck his cock.

But maybe she didn't know. Maybe I just *wanted* my mother to know, badly for her to know, so I gave her knowing it without asking her if she knew all of it. I gave her wanting to kill somebody—her husband for having sex with her child or her child for having sex with her husband.

But I was dead already, in that incest way of being dead. My mother walked through the streets of Brooklyn and into her death without ever telling anybody what it was like to know that her son was sucking her husband's cock. And because the sex makes me look at my stepfather more as an entity than as a human being, I see him alive and dead at the same time. He's a baffled premise on a darkening ring of memory having a half-life on a dusky, earthly plane, living far away from the world of whole people. I can barely see him through the steam of the afterlife.

Death can furnish the feelings of betrayal with their opposite feelings of compassion, and so I think how hard it was for my stepfather to get through a day without complicating it with regret. And how, like my mother, he slept so much to bear it. He was, I think, just living to be dead.

No stepparent is a true authority figure by nature of their designation. They're understudies, stand-ins. If there's any sex in the mix, it's difficult to enforce any law because no rules are ever taken seriously. How can somebody whose cock you're sucking tell you a friend can't sleep over? Sex erases all supervision with languid submission. And submission got traded between us like a fan during a ceremony in which there wasn't enough air.

Submission made it so that my stepfather didn't have very much currency during sex. He wasn't physically abusive in a way you'd expect an adult to be with the child he was interrupting. He softened inside the fragments we held together. The idea of two naked male bodies was something new to him.

Because my stepfather's sexual prowess was smoothed out by my innocence, his ejaculations were ordinary and unelectrical. The come didn't shoot out of him, but seemed to leak out like drool from the corner of a mouth. Or it dripped free, like oil from an engine. Everything got played out against the backdrop of his orgasm. Had I reached the age of orgasm yet? I can't remember. Had I started masturbating? I can't remember. I can't remember the reel of sex, just the splices where it got added.

My natural father threw me in the ocean to teach me how to swim. That was how it was with sex. I was thrown into the room with my stepfather. After I was thrown into the room, my stepfather and I didn't kiss or speak. The engagement was anonymous, and that pull of anonymity grew into the tension between pure illusion and erotic core belief. This was the beginning of that anonymous world I visit. This was where sex bloomed in the park and raced even harder in summers like a chemical through a public pool, where sex lit up steam rooms and train stations and even followed me and a stranger once into the stall of a thoroughbred racing star.

I resented my stepfather for a long time. Then just yesterday, my sexuality found a cadence that beat on without his influence. He was fucked-up in a lot of ways, but there were things about my stepfather that almost made him beautiful. Everybody has something that keeps them from blowing up. Music, for instance. My stepfather had great taste in music. And it smoothed him out because he was nervous most of the time. He was between medications, between examples of being loved. Then he was dropped, hated by some people.

When he couldn't be with people, my stepfather used to listen to music in the dark, as though it was a resort for the betrayed. The music was a bandage he held over his eyes and over his nervousness. It wasn't important who was making the music, just as long as they didn't stop playing.

When he died in 1990, I think my stepfather had stopped listening to music for a long time. He was very crazy and had to be calmed down a lot by the hospital staff. And when my brother called me up to say that my stepfather had died, I wanted to be relieved, almost happy. All my years of living with him had been so skewed and nerve-wracking and violent and otherwise. I wanted my stepfather's death to mean that something was all over for me too. But something was just beginning with my stepfather's demise. Something surprising. I forgave him. He wasn't an abusive or violent person anymore the way I'd expected he always would be. Even in death, in memory. And I couldn't stop thinking about how much music there was in that patent failure of love and how music always seems to rise above what people do to ruin their lives. Listening to music was a way to becoming a better person. Even if it never succeeded totally, music put you on a path. It was a miracle of singular grace being given the music, and an answer to the question of my stepfather's legacy, I suppose—if one is really allowed a legacy like this.

One thing I do know is something my stepfather also knew—that you can hear the music of love without knowing what the music is. And in this way, you lived.

A Dream: Who He Is
Will Be Him

Sometimes, when there's a chill in the air and the sun isn't falling on everything the way it can in the height of summer in a boat, in a chair, in the aluminum afternoon, he longs for something else inside the love he already has for his life and the life of his new partnership. It's not the *outside* love he wants. It's something that almost hasn't been expressed—the secret life, maybe, of love—something that is felt but not totally understood until there are moments of less light falling in the yard, into the pool, onto the surfaces of the outdoor furniture. He started living in a suburb the month the planes crashed into the buildings in New York. And while he worked alone at home, at the kitchen table, there was the secondhand sound of life coming from the other room—the woman who also lives there, people in and out from the city and some of the other suburbs. He was alone, but he didn't feel alone. He felt like the afterglow of being alone. Soon he will be moving away to a bigger city, with the man he loves to be alone with. And his aloneness will turn the corner. While the man he loves is away in the mornings and afternoons, he will be at a different kitchen table and out of the old range, the old sound of life. But soon he will find out something

about himself that he didn't imagine—the part that actually thrives in the room with him—the sense that he
is his own, whole person who had more love to give
than he could ever imagine. It will feel like a conversion
experience. In this way, he will become a city person.

Sometimes the man he loves forgets what it's like to be
loved. He listens, but he listens with regret—like the
old listening. The man that he loves is grieving over a
man who got lost a long time ago. And because this is
such a new relationship for him, he doesn't really question each new event but just falls into it, heart first,
headfirst, which is a surprise for him. A long time ago,
but not in the past, he used to be very careful when he
was breathing and now he just takes it for granted. He
is free, in that way, with the man who is grieving over
another man who got lost a long time ago. In the air, in
the country where he lives, everything is on fire. It
seems some days that the whole country is on fire and
the heat that reaches him is just a small picture of
something much bigger happening. The heat and the
love he has for the man who is grieving catch up to him
on the hot days and bring back, at times, his old life.
He breathed in his old life, but it wasn't breathing that
made him as alive as he is alive now. It was *the-life-
before* breathing.

Here's what I love about him now: he keeps letting more and more of himself out of his old self bag. He keeps moving love in different directions. He can see his shadow, and when he doesn't have a sentence, he can live in his shadow and not diminish himself the way other people can. He is sexy, the way ideas are sexy, but also he has a great and liftable body. I love his head and the feathers in it. And his eyes, his eyes, the eyes. There was a scene once that I saw in his eyes. Someone—was it me?—was touching the hem of an angel's gown.

I don't like to test him. I like to enjoy him and watch the day and night cover him with humor and patience and original ideas. But this love is so different than loves that came through the heavy doors of stopping drinking and wanting to write about my life that I sometimes get into the strange habit of touching it, pushing it into something it didn't originate, to make sure it is still there. To make sure it can survive discordance. It's delicate like a web though. Love that is so strangely new. He is sturdy and able to pass through moments without making them big and wanting. I feel his love too much, sometimes, and want to take my past life and my life with him in doses we can afford. He isn't like anybody I ever knew. He is all the way inside his body. He listens to me at night, when I have to touch our love life bruskly at times. And he's there the next morning, when the touch wasn't enough to knock the web down.

One time, one Saturday or Sunday, one time near the beach, in Plymouth, Massachusetts, specifically, down a little road and into his mother's house, and up a little flight of stairs to a sleeping loft and a little television light still spilling around and a little wind coming through the window, I got up from the bed and him and went out to have a couple of smokes. The air was thick, like it was holding something wet, but not threatening—not weather-something. There were too many lights from the other houses to make out the sky right, but the grass was sweet and cool and the cigarettes tasted good, like they do after a meal or at the beach after a swim. While I was there, away from the bed and him, back in the world of what keeps happening without us, I thought a lot about how much I loved him, even when I was confused by something I felt or did or said or confused by him. I thought of him that night as a kind of incredible light that lights up himself and also everything around him, and then what's left falls onto me. He has this beautiful energy about him—like the world is all about ideas that he might not be having. He's humble in that way, antinarcissistic. And I was only there, with the cigarettes, and he was this kind-of-light thought—only there, back in the world, away from his touch, for five or ten minutes, but I missed him. And in a good way you can miss somebody—I missed hearing what he might have said next. When I got back to bed he said, "Sometimes you can miss somebody more when you know they'll be back in five minutes than you do when they won't be back for a long time." *That's what I was thinking,* I thought, when he said this. That's what the dark and the cool grass were sending up into me. But I didn't tell him this. I didn't want him to know how much I missed him for only five minutes. I didn't want my boyfriend to think that I needed his love as much as I thrived on it. I wanted him to think that I was really good about time and what it takes away and shimmers back with.

Another time, in the first dusk that signaled summer was close, we were leaving a barbecue in Provincetown and walked our bikes up a little path that ran in the middle of some brush. We were sunburned and light-headed, on our way back to the house to have a nap before going out again that night for a plunge in a hot tub and looking at the stars. While we were going up the path, he turned to me and said, "We're in the woods." It wasn't a big deal, but it was very delicate, as though he knew exactly that I would think what he was saying was delicate and beautiful—just the right thing to say in that moment of our being together. He usually thinks very carefully about what he says, but this was a moment, his mind and his heart and his beautiful eyes seeing everything in the world at dusk, where he didn't have to think about what he was saying. It was one of those moments where the present feels incredibly enough. And he just said it, the way you would say, "Wait up." *We're in the woods.* From that moment on, maybe, we've been in the woods a lot at dusk—not in a literal way, not in a leaving-the-barbecue-for-a-nap kind of way, but in the sense that our time with each other is very intimate. Close. Recently, he remarked on what an interesting expression that was: close. That some people will walk into a room and say, "It's close in here," meaning something about the quality of the air in the room.

Sometimes, in the early morning, we buy coffee and take our cups and sometimes donuts and sit on a bench on an island facing traffic. Everyone who lives in Manhattan knows there are islands on Park Avenue and Broadway—islands of trees and dirty stone to draw a line between downtown and uptown—islands where one can sit, like my boyfriend and I like to sit, and see two directions at once. He likes to talk about his childhood early in the morning. I'm not so much a morning person, but I am a morning listener. A good one. He talks about his father, the cop, and his brothers and his sister, and I can hear in his voice a kind of regret or maybe it's a resignation—something in his heart is pulling his voice down to a place where I can hardly hear it. But I don't ask him to talk any louder because my just barely hearing it is the way it's supposed to be this morning—it's the style of the story. I can hear him all right, it's just not the kind of all right I'm used to, I guess. There are a lot of things about him that I'm not used to, I guess, but that's part of why I love him so much. My friend Marie and I always talk about people we love as having that great quality of being able to just go from one idea to another idea—people who don't, like so many other people, just reiterate the obvious, tell stories you've heard in some form or another. He's like that—the idea kind of person. So my mornings are always doubly awake for me when I am with him because I can see the ideas fly across his eyes like little lights from the sun, or the gleam of sun off the cars, or something inside him that is trying to tell the morning something—maybe tell the morning, *I'm alive, like this, in love.* We have mornings where we don't have to say a real lot to each other. We're at that point of the relationship, I guess—mind reading you could call it, but I always think of it as deep comfort. I always was afraid before of silence from another person, but with him the silence always feels safe—as though we don't have to always talk about what we are going through, but just keep watching the other one go through what they are going through until we can't see them anymore.

In My Father's Arms: A True Story of Incest
Walter A. de Milly III

Midlife Queer: Autobiography of a Decade, 1971–1981
Martin Duberman

Widescreen Dreams: Growing Up Gay at the Movies
Patrick E. Horrigan

The End of Being Known: A Memoir
Michael Klein

Eminent Maricones: Arenas, Lorca, Puig, and Me
Jaime Manrique

Body Blows: Six Performances
Tim Miller

Taboo
Boyer Rickel

Secret Places: My Life in New York and New Guinea
Tobias Schneebaum

Outbound: Finding a Man, Sailing an Ocean
William Storandt